Skin, Tooth, and Bone:

The Basis of Movement is Our People

A DISABILITY JUSTICE PRIMER

Second Edition

Skin, Tooth, and Bone:
The Basis of Movement is Our People
A Disability Justice Primer
Second Edition

Sins Invalid. (2019). Skin, Tooth, and Bone: The Basis of Movement is Our People (2nd ed.). Berkeley, CA.

To see more of our work, visit sinsinvalid.org.
To purchase more copies of the DJ Primer, visit tinyurl.com/SinsShopping.

This Primer was created with input and labor from: Patty Berne, David Langstaff, Leroy Moore, Nomy Lamm, Stacey Milbern, Micah Bazant, Max Airborne, Aurora Levins Morales, Kay Ulanday Barrett, Akemi Nishida, Leah Lakshmi Piepzna-Samarasinha, Maria Palacios, seeley quest, ET Russian, Lateef McLeod, Sandie Yi, Lezlie Frye, Kiyaan Abadani, NEVE, Cory Silverberg, Lisa Ganser, Seema Bahl, Devi Vaidya, Rachel Gelman, Eden Amital, Todd Herman, Amanda Coslor, Eveline Shen, Shayda Kafai, Malcolm Shanks, Maura Kinney, Caitlin Carmody, Shira Hassan, Laura Mintz, Lauren Smith Donahoe, India Harville, Sofia Webster, Andraéa LaVant, G Gomez, Gordon Brown, Rafi Darrow, Blair Webb, Yema Yang, Haley Parsley, Karina Camarera Heredia, Mordecai Cohen Ettinger, Zahna Simon, Ashanti Monts-Tréviska, Rei Ga-wun Leung, Dany Ko, Bianca Laureano

Table of Contents

Foreword

**We dedicate this offering
to disabled, queer, trans, and non-binary
people of color who live in rebellion knowing
(as Audre Lorde put it)
"we were never meant to survive."**

Where We Come From

In 2016, we published the First Edition of this disability justice primer, initially released to the public at our 2016 performance *Birthing, Dying Becoming Crip Wisdom*. This context was fitting for the launch of our primer, as we were sharing hard won wisdom living as brown queer crips organizing within our communities, within multiple justice-based movements, with and for our unique bodyminds. It was also time for Sins Invalid to offer our organizational lessons, after 10 years of work contributing to the Disability Justice Movement. Following those painful months after Trump's election, when we saw the initial rollout of his white supremacist anti-immigrant agenda, we felt it was important to assert our vision for a future where all individuals and communities are valued and seen as beautiful.

We also do this work in a physical landscape that continues to shift —the planet is in the unpredictable spirals of climate chaos. Our species has done damage and our earth is hurting. We feel and know this, and seek ways to breathe a deeper level of care into our relationships and collective experience. We may, or may not, survive as a species, but can move forward in love for each other regardless of where we are going. This process ranges from a mourning grief at what we will lose, to a rage against the capitalist extraction system with its attending systems of exploitation and violence, and everything in between — all of which we feel as we shift to new meanings of disability justice.

What exactly is disability justice? you may ask. In creating this foreword, we considered giving a brief definition of disability justice. The truth is, we clear the path to make the path. As queer brown disabled people, we are forced to teach the basics — asserting that we, too, are humans deserving of human rights; that we have a collective history and future; and that we are not deviant or aberrant but an essential part of humanity. As other movements will recall, this is the very start of a long and hard fight. Many who identify as progressive or Left have yet to root out their own ableism. Some may believe the phrase *"better dead than disabled."* These ableist beliefs defy reality testing, but they persist. As we challenge white supremacy, settler colonialism, gender normativity and violence that targets trans people, we challenge able-bodied normativity. Through this clearing practice, we create Disability Justice.

The Primer's Structure

To us, the entirety of these words, images and suggestions for practice are our definition of disability justice. We also wrote these words while living our cripped out realities: we wrote while on commodes, while using heating pads, while on painkillers, while twisting in pain, while getting IV infusions, while in bed.

The book is organized with three components:

— "skin," the images that offer us mirrors and we wrap around ourselves
— "tooth," cutting thoughts from disability justice activists
— "bones," the structures that are central to our work

Over the past several years, Sins Invalid has convened a national network of disability justice activists and comrades for conversations on disability justice (thank goodness for technology!); we are forever grateful and we use this primer to signal boost their brilliance! You will find many quotes in this primer, incisive comments we have coined as "teeth" from these luminaries, as well as from participants in episodes of "Crip Bits," a live-streamed talk show where we dig into the juicy issues facing our communities. We also heard our communities' requests for concrete writings and tools to share within our connected movements, and have responded by commissioning new pieces that we are excited to share with you.

Ableism has framed us as unfit for grace, to be hidden from public view. But as the beauty of an infant is distinct from the beauty of a 5 year old, which is different from a 15 year old, or a 25 year old, a 45 year old, or a 65 year old human, no age has the exclusive corner on beauty. Similarly, no form has the corner on beauty. The images in the primer represent our "skins," the many looks that only we can bring to the world.

The bulk of the primer is made up of what we have termed "bones" for the purpose of this publication. Sins Invalid has organizational practices that we try to keep as responsive to our bodyminds as possible, and are central to our work. We offer them here so that you can benefit from our process and continue to build on what we have learned.

Join the Conversation

Nearly 15 years after its inception, disability justice remains an emerging practice. After the First Edition of the primer was released, we invited feedback on our ideas. We created a feedback survey where readers could express their responses to the material. All respondents said they found the primer useful, and many also shared that it was missing parts of what is important to them about disability justice. With this in mind, we added new pieces to this Second Edition, including an extensive glossary of terms; a timeline of key moments in the history of disability justice; an additional timeline of Sins Invalid's history; a whole section on Audism and Deafhood; and a call to action from the environmentally injured. These materials were written and edited by members of their respective communities. We also tried to make our language more accessible and less academic. We have a long way to go in creating a disability justice primer that is actually accessible to people of all different cognitive styles and abilities, and we will continue to challenge ourselves in this way as we commit to ongoing mixed ability organizing and cross-disability solidarity.

While most of these pieces went through an extensive editing process within our organization, the Audism and Deafhood section was written and edited entirely by D/deaf contributors without interference from hearing people. This is part of an ongoing process of building bridges and creating respectful relationships within and between Deaf and Disabled communities, with attention to the ways D/deaf people's language and expression have been controlled by hearing people and institutions.

Even with the new additions to the primer, we acknowledge that there are gaps in representation in this Second Edition, such as voices from Indigenous or Two Spirit communities, neurodiverse, Blind, asexual and leather communities, those who are HIV+ and people experiencing addiction, amongst others. We plan to reach out and build connections with these communities and others as we continue our work, and ultimately will create a Third Edition of the primer to amplify more communities who use a disability justice lens to view their lives, ableism, community organizing and/or movement building. As with the First Edition, we invite feedback on the materials included here. We hope you engage with the text through the lens of your own work, and please share your thoughts with us regarding the content, format, accessibility, or anything else. You can reach us at info@sinsinvalid.org or via social media.

Come, join us as we create disability justice.

In community,
Sins Invalid

What is Disability Justice?

Adapted from Patty Berne's
"Disability Justice - A Working Draft"

In recent years, on websites, on flyers and in informal conversations, we've witnessed people add the word "justice" onto everything disability related — from disability services to advocacy to disability studies. This is done without a significant shift in process or goals, as if adding the word "justice" brings work into alignment with disability justice. It doesn't.

What follows is a working draft definition of disability justice. This is a living document that grows and changes along with our emerging movement. It marks a point of departure rather than a destination. It is an invitation to those of us working on disability issues, to continue to support one another to find a language as powerful and expansive as our movement's vision.

We'd like to start off with a quote from Aurora Levins Morales' book *Kindling*:

> "There is no neutral body from which
> our bodies deviate. Society has
> written deep into each strand of
> tissue of every living person on
> earth. What it writes into the
> heart muscles of five star generals
> is distinct from what it writes in the
> pancreatic tissue and intestinal tracts
> of Black single mothers in Detroit, of
> Mexicana migrants in Fresno, but no
> body stands outside the consequences of
> injustice and inequality...What our
> bodies require in order to thrive, is
> what the world requires. If there is a
> map to get there, it can be found in the
> atlas of our skin and bone and blood,
> in the tracks of neurotransmitters and
> antibodies."

Next Stage in Movement Evolution

Prior to the Disability Rights Movement, if people with disabilities were mistreated, there were no legal repercussions. Most public places weren't accessible and it was expected disabled people would not participate in society. There was important historic work done by

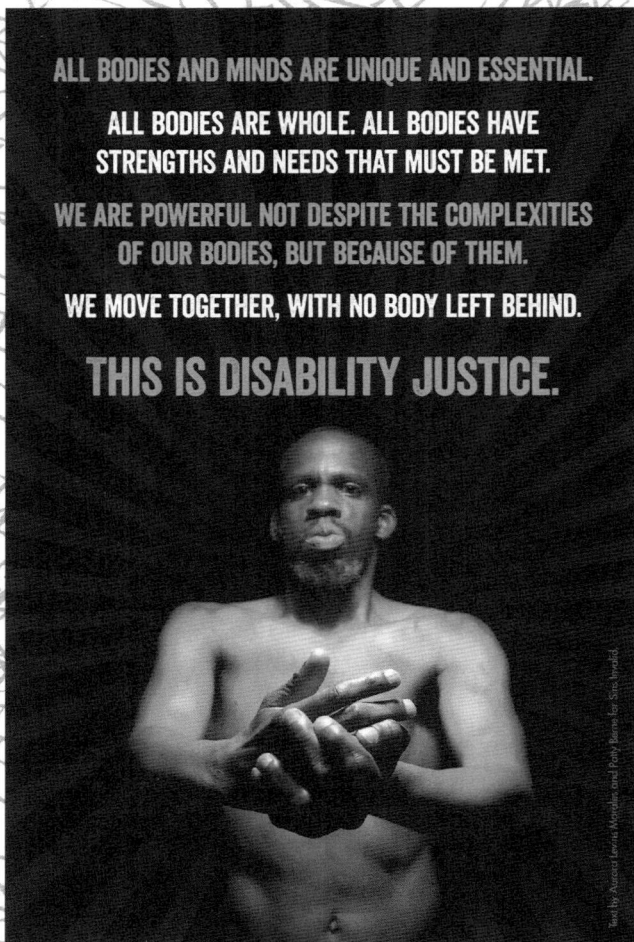

ALL BODIES AND MINDS ARE UNIQUE AND ESSENTIAL.

ALL BODIES ARE WHOLE. ALL BODIES HAVE STRENGTHS AND NEEDS THAT MUST BE MET.

WE ARE POWERFUL NOT DESPITE THE COMPLEXITIES OF OUR BODIES, BUT BECAUSE OF THEM.

WE MOVE TOGETHER, WITH NO BODY LEFT BEHIND.

THIS IS DISABILITY JUSTICE.

[Image description: The photograph shows black disabled activist and artist Leroy Moore. He has short cropped hair, a mustache and a beard. He is standing bare-chested, with his hands together out in front of him. The text above him reads: "All bodies are unique and essential. All bodies are whole. All bodies have strengths and needs that must be met. We are powerful not despite the complexities of our bodies, but because of them. We move together, with no body left behind. This is disability justice." Photograph ©Richard Downing; text ©Aurora Levins Morales and Patty Berne; courtesy of Sins Invalid] disabled people and allies to develop disability rights in the U.S., and it had many successes in advancing a philosophy of independent living and opening possibilities for people with disabilities. The US Disability Rights Movement established civil rights for people with disabilities. Like other movements, the current Disability Rights Movement includes advocacy organizations, service provision agencies, constituency-led centers, membership-based national organizations, as well as cultural and academic spaces.

And, like many movements, it is a product of its time and left us with some "cliff-hangers" that have yet to be resolved.

- Disability rights is based in a single-issue identity, focusing exclusively on disability at the expense of other intersections of race, gender, sexuality, age, immigration status, religion, etc.

- Its leadership has historically centered white experiences and doesn't address the ways white disabled people can still wield privilege.

- It centers people with mobility impairments, marginalizing other types of disability and/ or impairment.

WE ARE POWERFUL NOT DESPITE THE COMPLEXITIES OF OUR IDENTITIES, BUT BECAUSE OF THEM.

ONLY UNIVERSAL COLLECTIVE ACCESS CAN LEAD TO UNIVERSAL, COLLECTIVE LIBERATION.

THIS IS DISABILITY JUSTICE.

[Image description: A photograph of Black poet and organizer Cara Page, holding her hands out before her, leaning back, smiling wide. The text reads, "All bodies are caught in the bindings of ability, race, class, gender, sexual orientation, sexuality, citizenship. We are powerful not despite the complexities of our identities, but because of them. Only universal, collective access can lead to universal, collective liberation. This is Disability Justice." Photograph ©Richard Downing; text ©Aurora Levins Morales and Patty Berne; courtesy of Sins Invalid]

At its core, the disability rights framework centers people who can achieve status, power and access through a legal or rights-based framework, which we know is not possible for many disabled people, or appropriate for all situations.

The political strategy of the Disability Rights Movement relied on litigation and the establishment of a disability bureaucratic sector at the expense of developing a broad-based popular movement. Popular movements often begin when people develop political consciousness and name their experiences. Rights-based strategies often address the symptoms of inequity but not the root. The root of disability oppression is ableism and we must work to understand it, combat it, and create alternative practices rooted in justice.

While a concrete and radical move forward toward justice for disabled people, the Disability Rights Movement simultaneously invisibilized the lives of disabled people of color, immigrants with disabilities, disabled people who practice marginalized religions (in particular those experiencing the violence of anti-Islamic beliefs and actions), queers with disabilities, trans and gender non-conforming people with disabilities, people with disabilities who are houseless, people with disabilities who are incarcerated, people with disabilities who have had their ancestral lands stolen, amongst others.

In 2005, disabled queers and activists of color began discussing a "second wave" of disability rights. Many of these first conversations happened between Patty Berne and Mia Mingus, two queer disabled women of color who were incubated in progressive and radical movements which had failed to address ableism in their politics. Their visioning soon expanded to include others including Leroy Moore, Stacey Milbern, Eli Clare and Sebastian Margaret. These conversations evolved over time, at

> "Disability Justice is contextual, it's improvised, it changes. Just because a person has privileges here, depending on the climate or the governmental office or the housing situation, it shifts. Together, as a collective, our dynamics, moment to moment, each interaction is based on complication and nuance, and whatever equations or formulas we think that we may have down, they're going to pivot or shift together, depending on where we are together. Fuck systems and their shame."
> — Kay Ulanday Barrett

conferences, over the phone, formal and informal, one-on-one and in groups. While every conversation is built on those that came before it, and it's possible that there were others who were thinking and talking this way, it is our historical memory that these were the conversations that launched the framework we call disability justice.

Given the isolation enforced by ableism and capitalism, many of us have often found ourselves as leaders within our various communities, yet isolated from in-person community with other disabled people of color or queer or gender non-conforming crips. Many of us have found "liberated zones" online that celebrate our multiple identities. Disability justice is a developing framework that some call a movement. We are still identifying the "we," touching each other through the echoes of each other's hopes and words.

Given this early historical snapshot, we assert that disability justice work is largely done by individuals within their respective settings, with Sins Invalid and the Disability Justice Collectives based in NYC, Seattle, and Vancouver, B.C., being notable exceptions. These groups and organizing structures often come into being, fall apart and regroup with different names and configurations over time. Online groups like Sick & Disabled Queers can offer opportunities for people with disabilities to communicate and create new norms together. Some voices may emphasize a specific aspect of disability justice over another, which can be expected in all early movement moments. However, what has been consistent across disability justice - and must remain so - is the leadership of disabled people of color and of queer and gender non-conforming disabled people.

Disability justice activists, organizers, and cultural workers understand that able-bodied supremacy has been formed in relation to other systems of domination and exploitation. The histories of white supremacy and ableism are inextricably entwined, created in the context of colonial conquest and capitalist domination. One cannot look at the history of US slavery, the stealing of Indigenous lands, and US imperialism without seeing the way that white supremacy uses ableism to create a lesser/"other" group of people that is deemed less worthy/abled/smart/capable. A single-issue civil rights framework is not enough to explain the full extent of ableism and how it operates in society. We can only truly understand ableism by tracing its connections to heteropatriarchy, white supremacy, colonialism, and capitalism. The same oppressive systems that inflicted violence upon Black and brown communities for 500+ years also inflicted 500+ years of violence on bodies and minds deemed outside the norm and therefore "dangerous." Furthermore, racism, anti-Islamic beliefs, ableism and imperialism come together to feed us images of the "terrorist" as a dangerous Brown enemy, an "other" who is sexually and mentally "wrong." All this is compounded by the ways ableism, along with queer-hatred and the violence of the gender binary, label our bodies and communities as "deviant," "unproductive," and "invalid."

A disability justice framework understands that:

- All bodies are unique and essential.

- All bodies have strengths and needs that must be met.

- We are powerful, not despite the complexities of our bodies, but because of them.

- All bodies are confined by ability, race, gender, sexuality, class, nation state, religion, and more, and we cannot separate them.

These are the positions from which we struggle. We are in a global system that is incompatible with life. The literal terrain of the world has shifted, along with a neo-fascist political terrain. Each day the planet experiences human-provoked mudslides, storms, fires, devolving air quality, rising sea levels, new regions experiencing freezing or sweltering temperatures, earthquakes, species loss and more, all provoked by greed-driven, human-made climate chaos. Our communities are often treated as disposable, especially within the current economic, political and environmental landscapes. There is no way to stop a single gear in motion — we must dismantle this machine.

Disability justice holds a vision born out of collective struggle, drawing upon legacies of cultural and spiritual resistance. Within a thousand underground paths we ignite small persistent fires of rebellion in everyday life. Disabled people of the global majority — Black and brown people — share common ground confronting and subverting colonial powers in our struggle for life and justice. There has always been resistance to all forms of oppression, as we know in our bones that there have also always been disabled people visioning a world where we flourish, a world that values and celebrates us in all our beauty.

Discussion Questions:

- Why do disability justice activists say that a civil rights framework is a critical, but limited framework? When was a time that I saw someone being harmed, even though they are said to have "rights"?

- What do I see as the "next step" to create liberation for disabled people?

- Why must the Disability Justice Movement be led by disabled people of color, and disabled queer and gender non-conforming people?

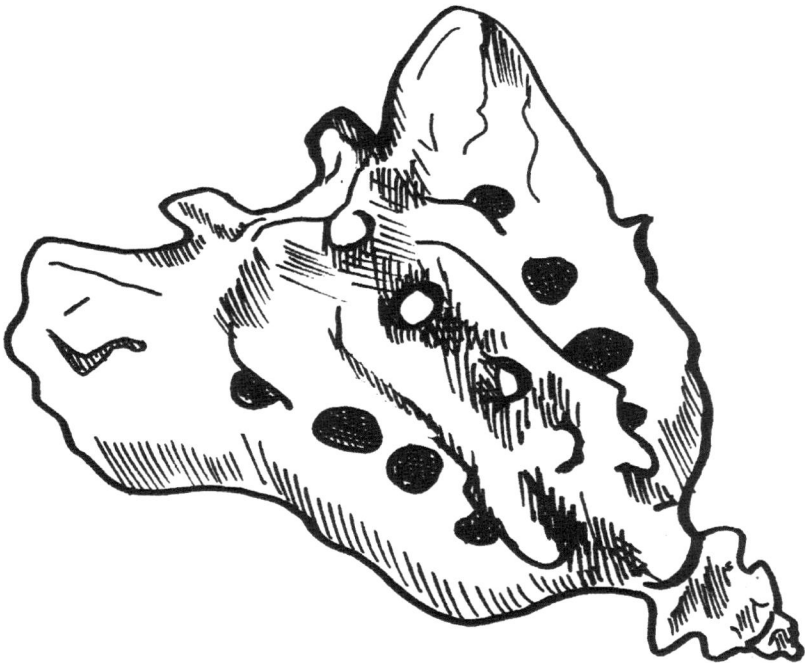

10 Principles of Disability Justice

From our vantage point within Sins Invalid, where we incubate the framework and practice of disability justice, this emerging framework has ten principles, each offering opportunities for movement building:

1. INTERSECTIONALITY

Simply put, this principle says that we are many things, and they all impact us. We are not only disabled, we are also each coming from a specific experience of race, class, sexuality, age, religious background, geographical location, immigration status, and more. Depending on context, we all have areas where we experience privilege, as well as areas of oppression. The term "intersectionality" was first introduced by feminist theorist Kimberlé Crenshaw in 1989 to describe the experiences of Black women, who experience both racism and sexism in specific ways. We gratefully embrace the nuance that this principle brings to our lived experiences, and the ways it shapes the perspectives we offer.

2. LEADERSHIP OF THOSE MOST IMPACTED

When we talk about ableism, racism, sexism & transmisogyny, colonization, police violence, etc., we are not looking to academics and experts to tell us what's what — we are lifting up, listening to, reading, following, and highlighting the perspectives of those who are most impacted by the systems we fight against. By centering the leadership of those most impacted, we keep ourselves grounded in real-world problems and find creative strategies for resistance.

3. ANTI-CAPITALIST POLITICS

Capitalism depends on wealth accumulation for some (the white ruling class), at the expense of others, and encourages competition as a means of survival. The nature of our disabled bodyminds means that we resist conforming to "normative" levels of productivity in a capitalist culture, and our labor is often invisible to a system that defines labor by able-bodied, white supremacist, gender normative standards. Our worth is not dependent on what and how much we can produce.

4. CROSS-MOVEMENT SOLIDARITY

Disability justice can only grow into its potential as a movement by aligning itself with racial justice, reproductive justice, queer and trans liberation, prison abolition, environmental justice, anti-police terror, Deaf activism, fat liberation, and other movements working for justice and liberation. This means challenging white disability communities around racism and challenging other movements to confront ableism. Through cross-movement solidarity, we create a united front.

5. RECOGNIZING WHOLENESS

Each person is full of history and life experience. Each person has an internal experience composed of our own thoughts, sensations, emotions, sexual fantasies, perceptions, and quirks. Disabled people are whole people.

6. SUSTAINABILITY

We learn to pace ourselves, individually and collectively, to be sustained long-term. We value the teachings of our bodies and experiences, and use them as a critical guide and reference point to help us move away from urgency and into a deep, slow, transformative, unstoppable wave of justice and liberation.

7. COMMITMENT TO CROSS-DISABILITY SOLIDARITY

We value and honor the insights and participation of all of our community members, even and especially those who are most often left out of political conversations. We are building a movement that breaks down isolation between people with physical impairments, people who are sick or chronically ill, psych survivors and people with mental health disabilities, neurodiverse people, people with intellectual or developmental disabilities, Deaf people, Blind people, people with environmental injuries and chemical sensitivities, and all others who experience ableism and isolation that undermines our collective liberation.

8. INTERDEPENDENCE

Before the massive colonial project of Western European expansion, we understood the nature of interdependence within our communities. We see the liberation of all living systems and the land as integral to the liberation of our own communities, as we all share one planet. We work to meet each other's needs as we build toward liberation, without always reaching for state solutions which inevitably extend state control further into our lives.

9. COLLECTIVE ACCESS

As Black and brown and queer crips, we bring flexibility and creative nuance to our engagement with each other. We create and explore ways of doing things that go beyond able-bodied and neurotypical norms. Access needs aren't shameful — we all function differently depending on context and environment. Access needs can be articulated and met privately, through a collective, or in community, depending upon an individual's needs, desires, and the capacity of the group. We can share responsibility for our access needs, we can ask that our needs be met without compromising our integrity, we can balance autonomy while being in community, we can be unafraid of our vulnerabilities, knowing our strengths are respected.

10. COLLECTIVE LIBERATION

We move together as people with mixed abilities, multiracial, multi-gendered, mixed class, across the sexual spectrum, with a vision that leaves no bodymind behind.

This is disability justice. We honor the longstanding legacies of resilience and resistance which are the inheritance of all of us whose bodies and minds will not conform. Disability justice is not yet a broad based popular movement. Disability justice is a vision and practice of what is yet-to-be, a map that we create with our ancestors and our great-grandchildren onward, in the width and depth of our multiplicities and histories, a movement towards a world in which every body and mind is known as beautiful.

[Image Description: Words of various fonts on a watercolor background with veins that look like trees, and layered clusters of bubbles that look like alveoli in the lungs. Text reads: INTERSECTIONALITY. LEADERSHIP OF THOSE MOST IMPACTED. ANTI-CAPITALISM. CROSS-MOVEMENT ORGANIZING. WHOLENESS. SUSTAINABILITY. CROSS-DISABILITY SOLIDARITY. INTERDEPENDENCE. COLLECTIVE ACCESS. COLLECTIVE LIBERATION. Text by Patty Berne and Sins Invalid. Design by Nomy Lamm.]

Access Suggestions for Public Events

What will make your event accessible, and who is it accessible to? So many things determine who shows up for an event, and who isn't able to, including free time, money, childcare, transportation, availability of interpreters, wheelchair access, use of fragrances, food options, and more.

This guide is intended to help organizers think through ways to include a spectrum of people (with and without disabilities) in your public event. Please note, these suggestions are not comprehensive! Each guideline will hopefully prompt folks to think through the multitudes of access barriers in the world and how we can best disrupt them to create "liberated zones" — areas where we aren't constantly suffering from disability oppression.

General Guidance Regarding Access

Access for all community members takes time as well as commitment.
If we want our gathering to be more accessible to more people, then think ahead! The longer in advance we consider these issues, the more

likely we can address them. Remember that improving access is always a work in progress and we all have to start where we are! So wherever we are at is a great place to start – we hope organizers will incorporate what they can from these suggestions, and then next time incorporate a little more. This is how we grow together.

We live in a capitalist, ableist world.
That means that, unfortunately, there is often a price tag that goes along with access. Individuals with disabilities should not be responsible for this cost. If you're an organization with a budget, pay attention to what gets prioritized. Know that some access needs can be expensive so create a plan to ask for financial support if needed, and find creative ways to make things work.

It's important to be non-defensive when receiving feedback.
We often reinforce and replicate ableism even when we are trying hard not to. Apologize, and work on finding solutions. Defensiveness creates unnecessary barriers. Sometimes people leave movements or communities, or stop attending events when they're met with defensiveness, so please be receptive to feedback and give thanks for the gift that it is.

Include access information on promotional material.

Access information is as important as information about the cost of tickets. Our promotional material should state what access needs have been addressed (i.e. ASL interpretation, wheelchair access, etc) and ask people to write or call to inquire about specific accessibility concerns. Asking people what they need to participate is a great place to start!

Everyone has access needs, and they can be talked about without shame.

It's okay, for instance, to verbalize a need to have a running heater, or a meeting location close to public transit. Practicing speaking up about our own access needs increases the likelihood that our needs will be met.

Access support can be shared.

Although some access needs, such as ASL interpretation, may require someone skilled in a particular field, other forms of access support can be done collectively. This can look like tag-teaming note-taking or taking turns preparing plates of food. Think about our own needs while also thinking of how we can help others with theirs.

Designate an Access Committee.

Also designate at least one or two Access Coordinators to address needs at the event.

The larger the group of attendees, the more important this becomes, because it gets harder to meet everyone's needs as they emerge. Have designated volunteers who can trouble-shoot and find creative ways to respond to challenges that arise.

Try to avoid isolating disabled people from our friends and communities.
If there is an accessible seating section, assume that not only people with disabilities will want to sit there, but our friends will as well. If there is a shuttle or van to help disabled people get from one place to another, assume that we will likely be in a group, and it's possible there will be more than one wheelchair-user in the group. Try not to let an access plan rely on the assumption that only one person will need an accommodation. If there is limited space, perhaps ask people to identify their party size ahead of time.

Have disabled people on the organizing team.
This makes accessibility a more organic process, identifying potential pitfalls early on, and shifting the idea that disabled people are only recipients of accommodation. Disabled people can create accessibility for each other.

Reflect on our own access needs.
Even if we have never thought of ourselves as disabled, we can think about our own access

needs and how they impact our experience of events. We can use our experiential knowledge as useful clues of what might be supportive for others.

Hold compassion for ourselves and everyone else in the process.
Sometimes, even with the best planning, some access needs go unmet. A little humility goes a long way in addressing the frustration that ableism creates.

Specific Access Items to Consider

Outreach
How are people going to learn about our events or gatherings? Some people respond best to visuals, some to text, some to audio, some to face-to-face interactions. Email and Facebook are useful, but perhaps we can incorporate phone trees, texting, and face-to-face invites. Organizers should plan to include an entire section in their outreach materials about access, and invite people to correspond with them with any additional questions.

Written materials
For visual accessibility, use plain sans serif fonts (like Arial or Helvetica), at least 14 point font, black ink on matte off-white paper. There are also fonts that are specifically easier for dyslexic and neurodiverse people to read,

including OpenDyslexic and Comic Sans. Create large-font (16 point or larger) and Braille versions of programs or handouts that can be available upon request. For colored text, make sure the text and background have high value contrast, instead of using bright colors of equal intensity (to check the contrast, try changing it to grayscale and see if you can still read it). Be aware that text reader software is unable to read some PDFs, so make text-only versions of materials available online as well.

Image descriptions

Text reader software is unable to read images, so make sure to create image descriptions for all photos, drawings, or graphics in online communication. These can be included with other text, inside of brackets with the label [Image Description]. Many platforms have the option of "Alt Text," which are short descriptions that text readers pick up on. If you are doing a Power Point or other type of presentation with visuals, describe all images verbally for participants. Image descriptions can include composition, style, colors, number and appearance of people, clothing styles, emotions, surroundings, and placement and transcription of text.

Audio Description

Audio describers narrate what is happening in a performance or film or work of art, for folks who are Blind or visually impaired. There are trained audio describers who can be hired to do description for events. If a trained audio describer is not available, find someone to describe the action without commentary, in order to provide informal description.

ASL and CART

Building relationships with Deaf community takes time and intention. Arrange for ASL interpretation and/or CART (live captioning), and include that information in all promotional materials. It's great to have both; while ASL can convey more nuance and feeling, CART captures what is said in text and can be useful for people who process information best in writing, or for D/deaf people who don't know sign language or have been systematically denied access to knowledge of their own language. Get recommendations to make sure the interpreters/captioners are trusted by the community, and provide interpreters/captioners with as much text ahead of time as possible, including spellings of names. ASL and CART are skills that require a good deal of training, so build it into the budget as an expected expense.

Microphones

If there will be more than 15 people in a room, plan to have a microphone and PA (public address) system so that people who are hard of hearing are able to follow what's happening. We know microphones can be intimidating to speak into, but they are very helpful. Remind people to wait to speak until the microphone is in front of them, and speak directly into it.

Bathrooms

Folks will need to use the restroom during your event. Trans and nonbinary people are often harassed or put in danger when they go into bathrooms. Folks with mobility impairments often cannot access bathrooms due to architecture. People with chemical injuries can become ill from scented soaps and cleaning products common in bathrooms. If possible, go to the site of the event, see the bathroom and speak with the management. Is there a toilet in a bigger stall that is lowered and/or with a grab bar for folks with mobility impairments? If not, see if there is a shop nearby with an accessible bathroom that will let people use it, and/or let folks know in advance of the event so they know to use the bathroom at home. Also understand that for some people, lack of accessible bathrooms will mean they cannot attend the event. Is there a gender neutral bathroom? If not, hang a sign on at least one bathroom that says "Gender Neutral" or "All

Gender Bathroom." Does the site use unscented soaps and cleaning products? If not, bring scent-free soaps to the event (Dr. Bronners is great), and offer to provide the venue with unscented cleaning products for them to use, preferably starting a week before the event.

Scents and chemicals

We can make events safer for people with multiple chemical sensitivities (MCS) by asking people to come to the event scent-free. This means avoiding all scented products, including commercial detergents, shampoo, soap, perfume, deodorants, lotions, fabric softeners, etc., before the event. Check out the space ahead of time to make sure it is free of air fresheners, scented soaps, and other scented products. Knowing that it is very difficult to assure a 100% scent-free environment, it can be helpful to create a scent-free area with hepa filters and fans helping to clear the area of scents, and then don't let people sit there if they are not scent-free. There are a number of online guides to help people become scent-free. Know that it is a process that takes some work before-hand, and offer as much education as possible. We like this resource because it is fairly simple and clear with lots of options of scent-free products: http://bit.ly/being-fragrance-free. Leah Lakshmi Piepzna-Samarasinha also has a great piece called "Fragrance Free Femme of Color Genius" that is searchable on-line.

Wheelchair and other mobility-related access

We've all seen the little blue wheelchair symbol, but that doesn't help to break down mobility needs. Good things to consider include: Is there a working elevator? Make sure you know where it is and can direct people to it. Are there steps or a steep slope in the building so that access may be limited? Is there carpet? (Carpet can be difficult for wheelchairs.) How far is Point A from Point B? Tell people how many steps there are, whether they are steep, whether there's a railing. If there are doors to open and close to enter the site, are they heavy? If there is a bell or buzzer, who will or won't be able to reach it? It can also be helpful to let people know about the terrain near the event. Is it at the very top of a very steep hill? Is there cobblestone or boardwalk? Is there a particularly pronounced crack in the sidewalk that people are likely to trip over? It is better to be honest and let people decide not to come, than to have people show up and then leave because it's not accessible.

Seating

Are there enough chairs for people? Are there wide, sturdy chairs without arms for fat people? What about chairs with arms for people who need that support to stand up? Are there spaces for people in scooters or wheelchairs to sit? Will these spaces allow chair users to sit with their friends and attendants? Is it possible for people to sit or lie on the floor if needed?

Food options
If food is part of the gathering, it's great to have multiple options – vegetarian, vegan, high protein (including meat), gluten-free, sugar-free, etc. Invite people to share their food allergies or dietary restrictions. Post ingredients somewhere visible and read them out loud before people start serving. If possible, let people know in advance if there will/will not be food for the group so people can plan accordingly.

Directions, Transportation, and Parking
How will people get there? If there's a rideshare list, make sure there's a space for access needs to be communicated. Is there public transportation? Share the specific bus or train lines and arrival times. Is the event during paratransit hours, and is there enough notice for people to be able to arrange for paratransit or other rides? Include the address of the event and clear directions in your outreach materials, including parking instructions, and put up clear signage at the event directing people to the most accessible parking spaces, pathways, entrances, etc.

Lighting
Fluorescent lighting can cause headaches, trigger seizures, and make spaces inaccessible for people with sensory or neurological disabilities. Consider bringing lamps to the space in order

to create more accessible lighting. Remember also that flash photography and strobe lights can trigger seizures. Tell people ahead of time if there will be any flashing lights in a film or performance, and give clear instructions to photographers that they not use a flash.

Quiet Space

It is helpful to have a low-stimulation space where people can go if they need to get away from the action. Designate a space where people can take a break if they are getting overstimulated or tired, and let people know how and when they can access it.

Video Conferencing or Livestreaming

Sometimes even with all your efforts to make a space accessible, there will be people who are not able to make it to the event in person. Make an effort to include people either by using video conferencing (Zoom is our current favorite), or livestreaming (Facebook Live is free). You can also hire people to do captioning for livestreams. Be sure to include a link for those who need it!

Schedules and Time Management

Be aware of time. It's important that people know the schedule and that you try your best to stick to it (with flexibility). Attention and information processing needs, pre-scheduled transportation, attendant care, childcare and more can impact people's ability to stay for the event. We can never assume people can stay an hour later if we're running late! If there has to be a schedule change, let people know and be as clear about it as possible.

Language

Everyone communicates in the way most familiar to them. When inviting people to the gathering or having a discussion, think about who will understand what's being said. Are the words being used familiar to most people in attendance? Explain your terms. Check in with folks – are interpreters (e.g. ASL, Spanish, Tagalog, etc) needed for the event for community members who have a language other than English as their first language?

Names, Pronouns & Access Check-ins

If it's a small enough group to do a full go-around, ask people to share their names, pronouns (if they wish), and access needs. (If people don't have specific needs they want to share, invite them to say "my access needs are currently being met"). If it's a large group, ask people to share their names when they speak. Offer name tags and invite people to write their pronouns along with their names. We can't assume what pronouns people use (he/him, she/her, they/them, or other non-binary pronouns) just by looking. Likewise, we cannot assume that people are able-bodied just because they look that way to us. Offer opportunities for people to identify their access needs and don't expect people to disclose their disabilities or diagnoses to you.

Transparency

Be upfront about remaining known barriers and stay in conversation about access as you learn more information.

As you can see, this is an ever-evolving process, and we learn and get better as we go. Mistakes are opportunities for growth! Now is the time to start expanding. Good luck, and we welcome reflection.

Access Suggestions for Mobilizations

These recommendations are to be used in addition to/in conjunction with the Access Suggestions for Public Events. This work is ideally done from a deeper political commitment to disability justice, or at least a critique of ableism and an understanding of disabled people's autonomy and right to consent. Know the difference between useful access support and patronizing ableist abuse!

Always have at least one Accessibility Point Person.
Announce them from the mic; have them wear armbands for visibility. Their skills should include a disability justice framework, problem solving, and good listening.

Create a clearly marked scent-free area.
Have volunteers who can help explain what it is and why it is important.

Create large-print and Braille versions of written materials.
Include important information, such as messaging/chants, route, destinations, National Lawyers Guild phone number, and

additional instructions. Use a "sans serif" font for readability (these are fonts without the little "tails" at the edges of the letters). OpenDyslexic and Comic Sans are fonts that are more accessible for people who are dyslexic and/or neurodiverse.

Use microphones for all instructions or announcements.

Provide ASL interpreters stationed at the mic, as well as throughout the crowd if possible.

Organize and announce from the mic:
- Availability of manual wheelchairs for people who need them
- Low stimulation spaces near the main gathering space (a room or a tent)
- Childcare and changing stations
- Multilingual translation options

Have people who know what's happening clearly marked.

Have them spread out throughout the mobilization (at the front, middle and back of the march, throughout the four quadrants of the rally, etc.)

Rent walkie-talkies.

More communication = more information = better access. Be mindful that police escalation will need to be communicated with participants in a calm manner, and will impact some more than others, particularly Black and brown people, under-documented people, and people with disabilities.

Provide seating (folding chairs, mobile bleachers, etc.).

Provide seating for rallies/gatherings where people can expect to be standing for any length of time. Announce their location from the mic and explain that they are for people with disabilities, elders, and others who cannot stand for a length of time. It is also useful to create an area for D/deaf people to sit together near the interpreter.

At a march:

Do a run-through of the route with mobility in mind ahead of time.

Keep an eye out for metal grates, grassy areas, hills, holes, cracks or curbs that will be hard for wheelchairs or scooters.

Invite people with disabilities to set the pace of the march by leading it.

Let people know that this is happening. Station people at the back of the march who are responsible for making sure that nobody gets left behind.

Give a verbal description of the march route beforehand.

Announce the destination and distance of the route.
This lets folks choose to meet the march at its destination.

DO NOT "direct" folks with mobility impairments to where you think they should be.
Offer respectful suggestions; no one should be hurried along; no one should touch people or their mobility devices without their consent.

Organize cars or vans to drive elders and people with disabilities along the route.
Include these vehicles as part of the march, if possible.

Provide seating at the destination.

Have a team whose sole focus is the safety of the participants.

Involve police liaisons.
Police liaisons should communicate to police that there are participants with disabilities (and elders, pregnant folks, etc) and that the march intends to respect their pace.

Be aware that cops will often target folks with disabilities.
Cops may perceive folks with disabilities as "weak links"; cops target folks at the end of actions as energy dissipates.

A note: Since we originally created these suggestions, the landscape in which we exist has shifted — it feels like we have an ever-increasing cascade of horrors facing us on the daily. We have a presidential administration that has proven time and again to be hostile to marginalized communities. Furthermore, our planet is experiencing climate chaos and is on the brink of collapse. In these trying times, life is precarious. Dire circumstances require creative strategies and responsive agendas. Much action is needed, and everyone has a role. Developing relationships with people with disabilities and asking us what we need is key. Inquire about where your body can be most useful in interrupting fascism, protecting immigrants, closing concentration camps, ending police brutality, honoring Indigenous sovereignty, and safeguarding the future of the planet and all its inhabitants. Invite us, strategize with us, bring all your skills and strengths. Don't forget us. We are central to this movement and the future we are creating together.

Sins Invalid Statement on Police Violence

In outrage and solidarity, we offer the Sins Invalid Statement on Police Violence, originally released on September 4th, 2014 to coincide with the Stop Urban Shield rally and noise demo in Oakland, CA. It was then released again in December 2015 when Mario Woods, a young Black disabled man, was shot over twenty times by San Francisco police while slowly walking away. In horror and sadness, we updated and re-released it in June 2017 after the death of Charleena Lyles, a pregnant Black mother with a mental health disability, who was killed by Seattle police in her own home after calling to report a burglary. Charleena was murdered in front of her children, one of whom has Down Syndrome.

Sins Invalid is a disability justice-based performance project centering disabled artists of color and queer/gender non-conforming disabled artists. Our work celebrates the embodied humanity of disabled people, and we understand all bodies live in a multitude of very real social, political, economic and cultural contexts.

[Image description: Watercolor painting of a young Black man's face and shoulders. He wears a black beanie and a black sweatshirt and has a goatee. He is gazing intensely at the viewer. Large handwritten text above him says "Justice for Mario Woods." Handwritten text to his left says "Over 50% of people killed by police are disabled." Handwritten text to his right says "No comprehensive federal data is collected, but available reports show at least half of those killed by police have psych disabilities. These statistics do not include people with mobility, sensory, or developmental impairments or people who are otherwise neurodivergent or sick/chronically ill." Handwritten text on his sweatshirt says "Disability Justice Now" and "#BlackDisabledLivesMatter." Art by Sins Invalid and Micah Bazant]

As an organization led by disabled people of color and queer/gender non-conforming people with disabilities, we live with high rates of state violence, from forced institutionalization, to ongoing police brutality and the murder of Black and brown disabled people.

We witness the horror of a deadly chokehold placed on Eric Garner, a Black man with multiple disabilities, by the NYPD. Our hearts break for Kayla Moore, a fat Black schizophrenic trans woman suffocated to death by police in her home in Berkeley, after her friends called 911 for help. (Similar to Eric Garner, Kayla's killers tried to blame her death on "obesity.") We are outraged by the in-custody death of Lakota 24 year-old mother of two, Sarah Lee Circle Bear, who was refused medical care; her last words were "I'm not faking." We embrace the memories of Victoria Arellano, an under-documented Latinx trans woman, and Johana Medina, an asylum-seeking Latinx trans woman, who were both living with AIDS, and died in ICE facilities as a result of being denied medical care. We feel devastation with the family of Natasha McKenna, who cried "You promised you wouldn't kill me!" just before being tasered to death by half a dozen guards in a Virginia jail. We stand with Lashonn White, a Deaf queer Black woman who was running toward police for safety, and was instead tased by police and jailed for three days without access to an interpreter. And we embrace survivors Andre Thompson and Bryson Chaplin, two Black brothers who now have permanent disabilities because a racist white police officer in Olympia, WA shot them multiple times each for attempting to steal a twelve-pack of beer.

We know that modern day police forces are direct descendants of the "slave patrols" created to police and control the bodies and labor of enslaved African people and violently repress their resistance to slavery. We recognize that Black, Indigenous and people of color with disabilities are pipelined from "special education" to incarceration of one form or another, and that more cops in schools means more police terror, especially for disabled youth. We acknowledge that people Native to this land are among the highest targeted to experience police terror and that the horrifically high number of Missing and Murdered Indigenous People is a form of state violence.

We know from experience that disabled people who are Autistic, who are D/deaf, who live with mental health impairments or cognitive impairments, epilepsy or movement disorders, are at highest risk of being assaulted by police, and that this is deeply compounded when we are further marginalized by homelessness, violence against trans people, and white supremacy.

CHARLEENA LYLES

#SAYHERNAME
BLACK DISABLED LIVES MATTER
BLACK MOTHERS MATTER

[Image description: Black and white charcoal drawing of a Black woman with long hair, looking directly at the viewer. Text at the top says "Charleena Lyles" in bold black letters. Text at the bottom says: "#SayHerName, Black Disabled Lives Matter, Black Mothers Matter" Image by Micah Bazant.]

SOLIDARITY STATEMENTS

We do not see training as a viable solution, since it leaves intact the fundamental belief of the police that their purpose is to "control the situation." As people with disabilities, our bodies and minds are not controllable and cannot always comply — this must be understood. Our bodies and minds are not criminal. We are unique and we celebrate our complexities.

We strongly oppose Urban Shield and all programs that seek to militarize police departments through paramilitary training and military equipment, as they serve to further dehumanize communities of color and poor and working class communities as "domestic enemies." Increased militarization of the police leads directly to increased police violence, particularly against disabled people of color.

We grieve that people with disabilities have largely been ignored and dismissed as key leaders in resistance to state violence by the US Left, silencing our stories and maintaining barriers to a united front.

It is within the context of disability justice that we demand that ICE (Immigration and Customs Enforcement) be abolished. No extent of reform can humanize an agency designed to criminalize migrants, deny their humanity, and profit off their detention and suffering. It is within the context of disability justice that we call for an end to the Prison Industrial Complex, including policing, surveillance and incarceration. It is within the context of disability justice that we align ourselves with Transformative Justice, a vision and emerging practice that seeks to address violence by holding people accountable within our communities and putting the power back in the hands of those most impacted.

"We can take a particular kind of leadership, and the bigger our goals for ourselves, the more we ask for, the more potential we have for doing that across many movements... For example, accessible public transportation puts you directly up against the oil companies who have a vested interest in automobile transportation. Who else is up against oil companies? The indigenous people in Ecuador who are fighting Chevron, people in Nigeria who are up against Royal Dutch Shell, the people in the Gulf dealing with the BP spill... The preciousness of our bodies and our lives is the basis for a huge coalition."
— Aurora Levins Morales

Disability Justice for Palestine

This statement was released August 6, 2014, during a 50-day military bombardment of Gaza by the Israeli Defense Force which killed over 2,200 civilians, wounded approximately 11,000, and destroyed over 20,000 homes. During this time, we were scheduled to premiere our newly released documentary at the Vancouver Queer Film Festival, which included an invitation to be a prominent speaker. However, we learned that the festival had accepted advertising from an organization known for "pinkwashing," i.e. promoting the gay-friendliness of the Israeli government in order to downplay the occupation and mass murder of Palestinian people.

At the time, our organization included many people of color with intimate connections to genocidal violence, and a number of Jewish people. There were two voices within the core of the Sins Invalid crew for whom the conversation held particular weight, a SWANA Muslim person and a Jewish person of color, and whose personal investment helped guide the group toward putting our politics into concrete action. Through a couple weeks of talking, crying and strategizing night after night, we realized that we could not in good conscience move forward with our plan to attend the festival, and released this statement, along with a "Disability Justice for Palestine" video and the "To Exist is To Resist" graphic, expressing our solidarity. We present it here as a document of that history, and as a continued commitment:

Sins Invalid is a disability justice-based performance project centering disabled artists of color and queer/gender non-conforming disabled artists. Our work celebrates the embodied, erotic humanity of disabled people, and we understand that all bodies live in a multitude of very real social, political, economic and cultural contexts.

We cannot separate the sexuality of people with disabilities, and our right to sexual self-expression and human connection, from the rights of all people to access food, water, shelter, medicine, breath, sovereignty, and peace. We were proud of our work, and were excited to curate an evening of films and discussion for the Vancouver Queer Film Festival (VQFF), including a screening of our documentary film about our performances. It was a valuable opportunity for us to share our work with new audiences.

However, we were angered and disappointed to see the print ad accepted by the VQFF that attempts to portray the state of Israel as a friend to LGBTQ communities, particularly in the current moment as the people of Palestine are living through hell and dying in staggering numbers daily. We recognize that such ads are part of a global effort to "pinkwash" Israel's image, to persuade LGBTQ people in other countries that the privileges enjoyed by queer Israelis are reason enough to be silent about the inhumane treatment of Palestinians of all orientations.

Palestinian civil society has called upon the world to exert political pressure and moral persuasion on Israeli society through the nonviolent tools of boycott, divestment and sanctions, and we are answering that call.

As we write these words, the Israeli military continues to kill scores of Palestinian civilians every day in Gaza, including queer Palestinians. The Israeli military is disabling thousands of people, while it continues to bomb hospitals, fire on ambulances, and destroy disability rehabilitation facilities. Of the thousands wounded from this current assault, many will be permanently disabled in a place where the basic necessities of daily life are stopped at the border, and basic medicine – much less adequate medical care, physical therapy, and adaptive technology – is beyond reach. These newly

[Image description: A drawing of a Black woman in a wheelchair wearing the orange uniform of the incarcerated, she reaches out and clasps the hand of a woman in white sitting against a wall wearing a hijab, whose arm and leg end short of a hand or foot, and are wrapped in bandages. Through an empty window frame a plane and explosions are visible. Text reads, "Disability Justice means resisting together from solitary cells to open air prisons. To Exist is to Resist." Image by Micah Bazant & Sins Invalid]

disabled Palestinians have been described by some as a "burden" to Palestinian society. In fact, these are the Palestinians whose bodies most directly bear the burdens of occupation and state violence, and most obviously show its scars.

As a result of the ad, we have decided to withdraw from the program and decline to screen our film, Sins Invalid, at the Vancouver Queer Film Festival. We will be screening it at an alternate location in Vancouver on Mon Aug 18th at 7pm PST. All tickets purchased for the VQFF program will be honored at our alternate event. We urge the festival to consider that the issue is not about its lack of advertising policy, but about its unwillingness to acknowledge settler colonialism and the violent occupation of Palestine.

We urge Festival goers to stand with us by asking the Vancouver Queer Film Festival to agree to refuse "pinkwashing" funding in the future, and to stand in solidarity with all queer and gender non-conforming peoples, wherever they may live.

Reproductive Justice is Disability Justice

As we've been working on this primer throughout 2019, we watched state after state pass more and more restrictive legislation on reproductive healthcare options (aka the "abortion bans"). Much has been written about this ongoing struggle, which is still unfolding. We feel it is important to insert our voice, to address the particular impacts on disabled people of color and queer, trans and nonbinary people with disabilities.

We are enraged by the recent "abortion bans" that are targeting people's ability to make safe and autonomous reproductive choices throughout the US. This legislation impacts us all and especially harms women, non-binary, trans, and intersex people, and lands heavily on disabled people's body autonomy.

The violent control and oppression of people's bodies in the US did not begin with this legislation. We know this violent control began with exploration, conquest and colonization of Indigenous lands and practices, and through chattel slavery and dehumanization through torture of Black people. Violence and oppression is found in all the systems of the US. We have seen this through the infliction of boarding/retraining schools on Indigenous people. We have witnessed state-sponsored eugenic programs in 32 states and Puerto Rico. The forced sterilization of US citizens, prison inmates, disabled people, and immigrant parents are direct violations of human rights and choice. Violence and oppression looks like COINTELPRO and the "war on drugs" as well as the violent and unjust response to the AIDS crisis. We have seen state violence and

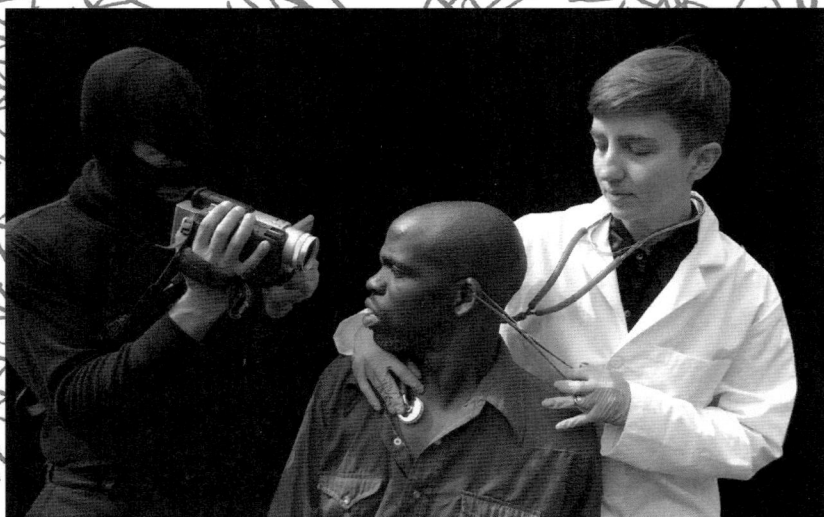

[Image description: A Black man sits with his head turned to the left. He is looking into a video recorder, which is held by a man who is standing and dressed in all black, including a black ski mask. To the right of the Black man is a person wearing a white labcoat, who is holding a pair of calipers around the man's left ear and holding a stethoscope to his heart. Pictured: Ralph Dickinson, Leroy Moore and seeley quest, photo ©Richard Downing, 2009.]

oppression in the constant undermining of Black enterprises and the rampant violence against Black trans women. Historical attempts to control "deviant" bodies show that reproductive choices must be understood as a human rights issue. Access to information, quality healthcare, and autonomy in decision-making are essential for the well-being of all.

Recent attempts to ban abortions have led to many non-consensual conversations about women, trans, and non-binary people's bodies. In these discussions, we must remember how disability justice values an intersectional analysis which requires us to consider the complexities of reproductive justice in the

"There is a lot of sexual violence that happens in the medical industrial complex. We are taught as disabled people from a very early age that we need to be compliant with those we are receiving care from. So fighting back against abuse goes against that lesson that we learned as children."
— Sofia Webster

context of ableism. Choosing when to become a parent is a basic principle of reproductive justice. On one hand, the fear of disability has been used as a tool to manipulate individuals' reproductive choices, sometimes causing people to opt for selective abortions to avoid disability, which is in line with eugenics. Simultaneously, disabled people have often been forced to terminate pregnancies under the pretense that we cannot be good parents because we are disabled. Additionally, because of the isolation of ableism, people with disabilities will be less likely to find safe options to terminate pregnancies when they choose. This context,

along with the struggle of disabled people to obtain comprehensive sex education and healthcare, means these abortion bans will be catastrophic for disabled folks.

Abortions will occur regardless if they are legal or not, but these laws are an act of violence particularly against poor and working-class individuals who will be unable to negotiate around the legislation and instead will be forced into unsafe practices to terminate their pregnancies. In some situations, pregnant people have already been criminalized and imprisoned for miscarriage or having been perceived to terminate their pregnancies, and these laws only continue to incarcerate more vulnerable populations. These laws specifically harm communities of color, as Black and brown people are always disproportionately impacted by criminalization.

These abortion bans may try to control our bodies, but women, non-binary, trans, and disabled people are not objects to be contained or manipulated. We are human beings that deserve care and choices, and we will not allow our autonomy to be denied. As such, we fully support reproductive choices that best suit each individual's context and needs. This is reproductive justice. We all deserve body autonomy, and to make the best choice for ourselves and our future.

Why We Commit to Mixed Ability Organizing

We all have bodies, hearts, and minds. We all have needs and capacities, strengths and vulnerabilities. A disability justice approach to mixed ability organizing means coming together across difference and inequality to build another, more liberated world. We work with and through the complexities and messiness that inevitably arise in this coming together. We patiently create new practices through conversation and experimentation, through trial and error. A disability justice approach to mixed ability organizing offers new forms of interdependence. We invest our energy in each other so that nobody is left behind.

Mixed ability organizing requires us to identify and bridge between different capacities, orientations, and relationships of power. It means paying attention to and being honest about the complexities of being in a body, and developing practices capable of attending to that complexity. For instance, while people with different disabilities may share a common experience of oppression under ableism, it can also be true that particular contexts can provide for the access needs of some and not others. A particular meeting space may present difficulties for people with mobility impairments, while a particular style of conducting a meeting may be difficult for people with emotional or cognitive impairments. These complexities play out not only across disabilities, but across race, gender, sexuality, class, and so on. For mixed ability organizing to honor the principles of disability justice, it must be able to take stock of, engage with, and work through these complexities.

A disability justice approach to mixed ability organizing asks more of people than simply acknowledging their oppression or privilege; it asks us to move beyond the disembodiment (state of being disconnected from one's body) that we have been socialized into under ableism. It doesn't help anyone to pretend that we don't have differing bodies, minds, and hearts, desires, needs, and limits — we most certainly (and fabulously) do. A disability justice orientation names ableism as a constructed, violent ordering of bodily difference that our movement works to unmask and undo, but it also recognizes that we currently exist in the world as it has been structured by ableism. Therefore, mixed ability organizing means engaging the tensions between living in this system (which categorizes us, limits us, disables us, and pits us against each other), while also resisting it. The tension between these two facts will be an enduring feature of the struggle for disability justice.

We must recognize that some forms of labor have been overvalued, while others are ignored due to their association with marginalized people's bodies and work. What does it mean to actively take stock of our capacities, our bodies, and our relationships to institutional power in relation to each other? Sometimes it means being honest about our physical, cognitive, or emotional limitations, and asking for the kinds of support we need. At other times it might mean challenging internalized ableism and embracing what our bodyminds do have the capacity for. Or it could mean learning to honestly identify and use our relative privileges in order to support collective access and disability justice movement-building. However, it is also important for those working within mixed ability organizing contexts to recognize the ways in which using our relative privilege can inadvertently reproduce the violence and hierarchies of ableism, racism, patriarchy, sexism & transmisogyny, classism, etc. The leadership of disabled people of color and queer, trans, and gender-nonconforming people with disabilities should always be at the center of disability justice movement building.

Mixed ability organizing means nurturing old and inventing new ways of holding and supporting one another. We lovingly depend on each other to support our struggles against a world that says we are each in it alone and that our oppression is our fault. We collectively develop awareness of our needs and capacities, of what and how we're giving and receiving, without getting into tit-for-tat accountings of our debts to one another ("I did this for you, so now you have to do this for me"). As the black radical poet and theorist Fred Moten might put it, these debts are truly incalculable. How could one possibly quantify the many ways we might lend our bodies, minds, and hearts in service to one another?

Mixed ability organizing also means being attentive to the ways that power plays out in our labors with and for one another, even as we try to create new forms of collective care. Who is doing what kinds of labor, how much, for how long, and how do these facts map onto gender, race, and other instances of difference and power, often in unacknowledged ways? For example, are female socialized or femme-identified people carrying the bulk of the emotional labor of the organizing? Have we come to imagine non-disabled people as the "givers" and disabled people as the "receivers" in ways that replicate ableism? Are people of color doing the majority of the work while white people receive more attention as "leaders"? Mixed ability organizing means working toward collective accountability rather than strict accountings — reciprocity rather than receipt. It means interrogating the ways power shapes the flow of our giving and receiving, without ever assuming that we could (or would even want to) "settle our accounts" or make everything balance out to zero.

Disability justice encompasses and embraces all bodies, minds, hearts, and forms of embodiment. This emergent movement is unquestionably of, by, and for disabled people of color and queer, trans, and gender-nonconforming people with disabilities, as we are subjected to the greatest violence of ableism, and therefore have the greatest stake in its abolition. Simultaneously, disability justice is ultimately about re-imagining and reinventing all of our relationships with one another, as well as with our own bodyminds. It is about transforming the very material and psychic frameworks that designate some bodies and minds as normative, valuable, and acceptable and others as deviant, worthless, or dangerous. We all have a stake, and role to play, in disability justice, in dismantling ableism and building toward a world where all bodies and minds are recognized and treated as valuable and beautiful. We still have a very long way to go, but we have each other to hold, and be held by, through the journey.

Principles of Mixed Ability Organizing

Or "From each according to [their] ability, to each according to [their] need."

— Karl Marx

Mixed Ability Organizing requires a commitment to:

- Valuing people as they are, for who they are.

- Valuing both the process and the products of our work.

- Knowing that Black and brown/queer crips bring flexibility and creative brilliance to our pursuit of accessible ways to engage with the world and each other.

- Exploring and creating new ways of doing things that go beyond able-bodied/able-minded normativity. We are well worth the effort it takes to create a mixed ability process.

- Valuing the insights and participation of all of our community members and therefore committing to breaking down ableist/ patriarchal/racist/classist isolation of people with disabilities. Isolation ultimately undermines collective liberation.

- Remembering that moving together doesn't mean we all move in the same way; valuing and adoring all the ways that we show up.

- Acknowledging that everything is not equally accessible for everyone at all times.

- Finding roles for each member of a community that are rooted in self-determination, active consent, and the needs of the collective.

- Recognizing the brilliance of our communities, and supporting and challenging each other to express that brilliance in ways that make sense for us.

- Challenging and dismantling the multiple systems of oppression that have socialized us to be comfortable with mere acceptance from, and assimilation into, an able-minded/ able-bodied normativity; being aware of the dangers of reproducing this complacency.

- Acknowledging that there is an iterative/ repetitive/cumulative process of supporting each other, developing our skills, and developing our leadership, meaning this is a constant process with many stages and we usually don't get it right the first time.

- Acknowledging that we all can act as allies to one another in different ways across abilities, but that we need to be intentional about our institutional positions and other types of power; making sure that we are organizing with, and not for, one another.

- Committing to our collective stake in ensuring access and striving to be accountable to each other; knowing that we will make mistakes, and asking each other for understanding and patience as we create this road together.

Audism & Deafhood

A Foreword

by Ashanti Monts-Tréviska

Deafness as a medical model and Deafhood as a cultural model mean different things to each Deaf individual based on their personal journey of discovering who they are through their own identity process. If we can understand how colonialism had an impact on various cultures, we can see how audiocentric narratives have colonized the bodies of Deaf people by taking away their collective power to reclaim their true identity. Dr. Paddy Ladd saw how the medical model of deafness have been inhibiting Deaf people from actualizing their deaf possibilities collectively based on the cultural understanding of oralism being the form of monocultural colonialism. Deafhood, on the other hand, was coined by Dr. Paddy Ladd. Ladd explained the exploration of Deafhood is a journey for each Deaf individual to discover the spiritual embodiment of self-authenticity.

On the other hand, disability justice advocates have asserted that their equitable citizenship have not been fully embraced. It is relatively easy to categorize Deaf people as part of the disability group, however, it has caused greater misunderstanding of Deaf people's cultural identities. Ladd clarifies this misunderstanding by stating that "the administrators of medical model adopted the term disability, which for the first time placed deaf peoples in an administrative category that included all other 'physically impaired' people. This had both positive and negative effects for deaf communities, who were unhappy about such a categorization primarily because of the disability movement's insistence that all disabled children be mainstreamed, which led to the closure of hundreds of deaf schools across the West." In clarity, Alex Lu of *Deaf People Don't Need New Communication Tools - Everyone Else Does* questioned why everything in the society have to cater to hearing people to maintain the status quo. Lu pointed out that Deaf people as cultural-linguistic (language minority) members are viewed as a liability in terms of communication, when in reality, they are not. Having phonocentric privilege leads the dominant group to practice audism as a socially constructed discrimination or bias towards Deaf people.

In that respect, my experience as a cultural-linguistic person (a member of language- and culture-oriented diversity) is equivalently important to see that I have both epistemological and linguistic privilege in some areas which means I have the ability to read & write English well as a speaker of American Sign Language (ASL). With self-awareness of my privilege, I am reminded that some Deaf people don't have this privileged experience of carrying English as a second language very well because of the varying educational experience. In understanding this, I have taken an accountability to share my knowledge and wisdom with Deaf people who I have crossed paths with when they are ready to embrace it. I don't impose my understanding of the nature of life onto them because I truly respect their personal journey and I trust their own growth process.

Rei Ga-wun's poems guide us to see their own relationship with English and the struggle to find inner peace as a Deaf person in the Asian culture. I have wondered if it would have made a difference if the world was conscious of the sacred process of being a cultural-linguistic person.

Rei Ga-wun's profound expression about audism can guide us to understand how people with audiocentric privilege can cause harm to Deaf people's collective needs for growth. Many people get confused about how some Deaf people do not identify as Disabled people. Rei Ga-wun reminded us that there are many Deaf people who are able bodied with sighted privilege which makes it easy to overlook the daily struggles of DeafBlind people and Deaf Disabled people within Deaf communities. Rei Ga-wun is guiding us to reframe our minds about how we view oppression when we speak of our own experience of oppression collectively.

Dany Ko offers an insight how ableism and audism are interdependent and interconnected with each other. Dany offers an insight on how Deaf community members and Disabled community members may not have a full understanding how multiple forms of oppression have on their communities because they have not had a critical discourse on what community care means to proactively dismantle multiple forms of oppression. Dany reminded us that their own understanding of social mobility means different things in different cultures, in different geological locations, in different biological environments and from different educational experience. In that cultural respect, Dany guides the reading audience to understand that Deaf community members do experience language barriers due to the audiocentric idea that the ability to speak and the ability to hear is the monocultural and monolingual status quo narrative that sets the standard of what is considered as normal.

Conclusively, Dany sets the tone that there is a need for both cultural and social solutions to bridge Deaf communities and Disabled communities together to reframe the meaning of human connection.

Enjoy the journey with us as we question the meaning of audism.

Audism

By Rei Ga-wun Leung

Audism

How do you define Audism?

When do you see Audism?

What define Audism?

A shearing raw form of everything in a
sugarbliss fast and moving pace.

A round or lines or cluster folx who passes you,
approach you, sees you, make you feel

Small.
Excluded
Uncomfortable
No support
No empowerment

Lastly, no voice

Small in fortune that is easily with their lips
brush with "nevermind, you don't need to
know."

That is one filling of the bottom- this bottle.

Just a layer coming forth in nature of what becomes.

Everything is auditory.

Everything you see is spoken, navigating knowledge why is it not okay.

As a anomaly- as a sheep nodding your head as the wolf hunts

As a puppet drawn on our strings attached no control lapse lapse lapsed

Access being denied

Voices block

Dragging yourself deep in roots, wondering these questions all to yourself.

To ask yourself such a simple following questions:

Oh~ how I love taking pop quiz or get to know yourself results,

Are you hearing?

Are you Deaf?

Are you white?

Are you BiPoC?

Do you sign?

Do you speak?

Do you write or speak English?

What if you are hearing?

What if you are Deaf?

What if you are Blind?

What if you are DeafBlind?

What if you are neurodivergent?

What if you are Queer?

What if you are gender non-conforming?

What if you are trans?

What if you are ableist?

What if you are disabled?

What if you are racist?

What if you are an empath?

What if you are violent?

Are you any of those?

Are you any of them?

Are you done?

A Deeper Review into Deaf Culture in a Hearing World

by Zahna Simon

Part of Audism that is highly prevalent in our society is Audism that is not obvious.

Growing up as a Deaf dancer, alone in the mainstream in a hearing world, I have seen the evolution and shifts from a time when society would not give me a chance if they knew I was Deaf—I would often complete bookings, wait until after class and show up to auditions before even mentioning I am Deaf as a means of proving myself equal to everyone else around me first...To now where people are actively searching for their "token" Deaf dancer to uplift themselves and prove that they are diverse especially if that Deaf dancer is also of a marginalized racial background. Often there's only been two options as a Deaf dancer which is either people being overly amazed by my ability and talent placing me on a high pedestal yet not actually hiring me because they are so amazed a Deaf person can actually dance to music that they don't see else past that or to be completely ignored, looked down on and/or considered "too much work."

People who are d/Deaf or having a hearing loss use a variety of terms to describe themselves. In this DJ Primer, we chose to use the term "Deaf," to embrace Deafhood as a cultural identity with its own traditions, art, history, values and behaviors that typically use sign language as a means of primary communication, vs "deaf," which only refers to lacking the sense of hearing.

The fact remains that d/Deaf people can do anything with no limits except literally "hear" in the same way that hearing people do.

I am blessed to work with an African American Deaf Director/Choreographer, Antoine Hunter, who says as I quote it "When hearing people do not take the time to listen to us, who is more deaf — us or society?"

With that said, the Deaf community are typically the last marginalized group to be thought of, in my experience, either society doesn't want to accommodate us, assumes our accommodations are automatically met and/ or assume they have the authority to think, speak and decide for us. In turn society with the "hearing" does not listen to us and we continue to be invisible unless we work extra hard to be LOUD. I call this, Hearing Take Over, when hearing people try to control the situation and impose what they think is best for Deaf person/people without allowing the Deaf person any input, to express themselves or the space and opportunity to lead thus opposing empowerment and sustaining Deaf oppression.

As you continue to read through the next pieces with an open mind, remember that enablement is not only providing opportunity to others with less access but also empowering those to lead and rise above you with full inclusion.

Level of Audism

By Rei Ga-wun Leung (2017)

Define Audism,

When everything is auditory based

That includes sounds, speaking, and information that is translated and enters and by pass with access

Deaf space

We are free when we form creativity ideas in our natural language

As condensed in some ways, we are restricted in reminders of our oppression

Oppressed will always and can be a oppressors.

To explain,

There is level of Audism

This applies to people who think Deaf people can't..

This applies people who don't sign,
and think sign are not okay.
This applies to when deaf people who have
ability to speak and grew up over time, and
speak upon deaf people who sign.
This applies hearing forget that we are Deaf.
This applies to Deaf people not able learn to
be in crisis of their identities and prefer hearing
dominant culture.
This applies to not acknowledging and listening
the concerns, feedback and that is "audism"
This applies to many of oppressors and
oppressed

What is
boundaries
And respect?

Step 1.

There is very often room of people who only
speak in auditory called hearies or hearing in a
better term.

In form of their mouth is so important, they meet
up with us and is hard to elaborate what they
are trying to say and trying to make us say.

Then comes in complexities where, deaf people
transition in the hearing world dominantly.

They haven't discover there is Deaf culture

and Deaf people around fully bloom in their identities.

They haven't found a community that are in their similar experience and lived experience.

Then there is people who are brought to believe devices that were meant to "fix" or "cure" is the obligation to feel we are "okay" and a passing to the hearing world.

Step 2.

Sourcing and exposing with Deaf culture and Deaf history in their world.

Collapse with two worlds: Deaf and hearing world.

Most of us feel in anguish, denial and defeat

Their identity is often in crisis

Their view begun to change slightly and this could lead to knowing that they have a choice to sign.

Step 3.

Continuing the language, and caring about what their identities... stable to them.

Some think only Deaf.

Some think of Deaf youth.

Some think of Deaf senior.

Some think of DeafBlind.

Some think of DeafBIPOC.

Some think of Deaf disability.

Some think of Deaf wheelchair user

Some think of Deaf Autistic

Some think of Deaf LGBQT+

Some think of Deaf immigrant

Some think of Deaf poor

Some think of Deaf religion

Step 4.

Relatively, most of us think just one.

How narrow our scope is to be.

When we don't realize that is greatly affecting others.

To deep root and analyze yourself in your whole being takes a lot of time and quality for yourself.

Step 5.

It gets harder when you realize, the amount of time you analyze yourself and think about others to really give space and elevate the power shifts happening.

We are our own- being of ourselves.

We do not have the same experience. And we can voice our own and share that particular experience.

Having to reclaim the space that was in your bubble sphere of your identity and world.

And if someone invades yours, is an ugly mixture in the crock pot.

Step 6.

As the oppressors leave, with no hope of validating the victim and their sway pride swoon over with audience that is in fascination and glory left the room.

If that was a flip in your story, what would the results be?

Can you handle the truth?

Can you handle yourself?

Can you still be you?

D/dEAFNESS

By Dany Ko

Deaf [/def/]: lacking the power of hearing or having impaired hearing (Merriam-Webster)

This definition focuses on *lack, loss, and impairment.* As we know by now, disability justice means focusing on what we *have and can do.* I prefer defining deafness as needing more than just auditory cues to communicate; it may mean using visual or physical cues instead, such as lip-reading or sign language.

Generally, to be deaf with a lowercase d is to be medically deaf or hard of hearing. To be Deaf with a capital D is to be "truly" Deaf; that is, a part of the Deaf community. Sometimes, those who are D/deaf do not identify themselves as being part of the wider disability community. Some do this in an effort to differentiate D/deaf culture, and others do it in an attempt to classify D/deafness as something other than a disability. As such, there are schisms within and between the D/deaf and disability communities.

AUDISM IN THE DISABILITY COMMUNITY

Audism [/'ȯ-ˌdi-zəm/]: discrimination or prejudice against individuals who are deaf or hard of hearing (Merriam-Webster)

Audism seems to be very common in disability community spaces. Sometimes this is due to the space itself, and other times it is due to the people present. While audism may be unintentional, it seems that many disabled people don't know much about D/deaf customs and culture. This leads to a miscommunication and unintentional disrespect.

Regardless of ability, here are some things anyone can do to accommodate for those who are D/deaf:

- Try to be quick and nonchalant when walking between two people communicating via ASL.

- Maintaining eye contact is not always possible for everyone. However, concentrating on an ASL interpreter rather than the D/deaf individual you are communicating with when you don't have to lipread or otherwise face the interpreter is considered rude.

- Some people need to lipread. Take into account the lighting of the room. Lean in when appropriate.

- It takes a large amount of focus at times to truly understand what someone is saying, which may result in D/deaf people making "weird" or "rude" expressions/noises.

- The polite way to get a D/deaf person's attention is by waving at them or even lightly tapping their shoulder.

- When possible, provide captions/subtitles. This can also include live captioning at events such as panels and meetings.

ABLEISM IN DEAF COMMUNITIES

Ableism [ˈābəˌlizəm]: discrimination or prejudice against individuals with disabilities. (Merriam-Webster)

It is shameful that the Deaf community has decided to distance themselves from the greater disability community widely due to ableism. Many claim that Deafness is not a disability, but rather, a way of being part of a different community and culture than hearing people. Yet, this excludes those who may not be able to use, learn, or adhere to ASL and Deaf customs. While D/deafness as a disability is a controversial topic, it is quite clear that ableism is rampant in the Deaf community.

If you identify as D/deaf, please have a clear

understanding of the following:

- To disable another person is to create barriers for them that make it harder or even impossible to navigate socially and/or physically. Leaving disabled individuals out creates disabling environments. No one should be promoting the oppression of other communities simply because they do not identify with them.

- There are many other ways of participating in the culture and community, even without using ASL.

- D/deaf people benefit from disability rights and justice movements.

- The Deaf community itself is not accessible. If D/deaf people truly want hearing or mainstreamed deaf people to learn ASL, then Deaf people should be accommodating those who sincerely want to learn about and join the Deaf community.

METHODS OF FORMING ALLIANCES, HAVING DISCUSSIONS

Alliance [/əˈlīəns/]: a bond or connection between families, states, parties, or individuals; an association to further the common interests of the members (Merriam-Webster)

I like this definition, as it promotes the idea of a bond, a connection. Perhaps it is because I am proudly both deaf and disabled, and I feel that connections between people and communities are extremely important to furthering general disability justice and liberation for all people.

Generally, the beginning to a good alliance starts with sincere conversation. Genuine connections can be made through an understanding of both sides and each others' needs. Thus, below are some discussion questions that I feel would lead to a better bond between the D/deaf and disabled communities. Hopefully, answering these questions gives an idea of how to move forward with creating alliances, bonds, and connections between the two communities.

Discussion Topics/Questions:

How do we define disability and disabling situations? How can we approach the topic with ableist D/deaf people and disabled people who do not understand why or how to accommodate for D/deaf individuals? What sort of training should activists, workers, panelists, etc. undergo?

What has, in the past, led you to practice audism/ableism? Recognizing our own contradictory, complex human natures is a huge step in understanding how we are socialized to understand disability and D/deafness and how we can avoid it later on.

In what ways do our identities and communities intersect and interact? There is no disability or D/deaf justice without intersectionality. Being able to understand the impact and interconnectedness of different identities, as well as shared experiences, is a step towards alliance.

How can we better accommodate for each other? What does it mean to accommodate for someone? What does accommodation and accessibility look like? Remember that it goes beyond merely accommodating for someone physically; accommodations can be mental, emotional, and even fiscal.

How can we move forward with the understandings we have generated? This is more than just understanding accommodation and promising to make a space or event accessible. This question asks how you can continue to improve yourself, your activism, and your work through what you have learned.

A Call to Action from Survivors of Environmental Injury:

Our Canary's Eye View at the Crossroads of Disability and Climate justice

By Mordecai Cohen Ettinger, Health Justice Commons & Sins Invalid

As people with disabilities we are all survivors. Many of us are survivors of state violence, targeted because we are Black, Brown, Indigenous, members of other communities of color, and/or queer, transgender, gender non-binary or intersex communities. Or, we've survived forced migration and survive the daily perils of anti-immigrant hostility and detainment. Disabled people are almost certainly all survivors of abuse at the hands of medical institutions and health insurers either through neglect, withholding of care, coercive treatments, or due to the dangerous ignorance of our bodies and health conditions. Finally, those of us with visible or invisible disabilities live under an unspoken apartheid in every place on the planet in which we face multilayered isolation, social rejection, stigma or threat of forced institutionalization.

What ableism hides, as does every interconnected system of oppression, is that our survival as disabled people instills us with powerful wisdom that is necessary now more than ever for our human and planetary survival.

You may have heard the saying "canary in a coal mine," referring to a bird that miners would carry down into the mine shaft with them; if harmful gas began collecting in the mine, it would kill the canary first, warning miners to get out. As survivors of environmental injury, we are planetary whistle blowers; we are the canaries in the coal mine that our planet is becoming after 500 years of colonist destruction and capitalist expansion. This expansion and exploitation of people and land has come at the cost of life itself. And so, we the canaries are called forth to sing our urgent song of truth.

Some of us are radiation poisoning survivors, others of pesticides, diverse classes of toxic chemicals and petroleum products, heavy metals, mold from neglectful landowners or construction practices, or climate fires and other climate related disasters. Many of us have been injured, made ill or disabled by several of the above, as toxic exposures are normalized in our everyday lives.

We are multi-racial, we are survivors of attempted genocides, forced migrations, transatlantic slavery, ableism, historical trauma, and ongoing intersectional institutional and interpersonal oppression – all the brutal forces that have treated people and the planet as useable and disposable.

Climate Justice is Disability Justice

The current climate crisis has collectively awakened us to the immediate need to cease our global dependance on a fossil- fueled economy. We know we need to go green fast.

As survivors of environmental injury we see another necessary path of action for our collective survival, still unseen and misunderstood by many: our planet has reached a toxic tipping point. We must stem this tide of toxins into our bodies, our communities, our ecosystems, our institutions and industries.

The facts tell the story as loud as the song of our bodies' suffering. According to the UN, in 2016 Europe alone consumed 350 million tons of chemicals, over three-fourths of which are known toxins.

In the US, 80,000-100,000 chemicals are used in industrial and consumer cleaning, construction, personal care products, and in our food supply. The exact number is unknown because according to the EPA, less than a fourth of these have ever been tested for safety by any independent research body. Over 75% of chemicals are "okayed" for use after the industries profiting from them claim they meet their corporate standards for safety.

In 2009, Black Women for Wellness and US Right to Know teamed up to generate research. What they found is that the average woman in the US, across race and class, wears over 60 chemicals per day in personal care products. Many of these are known endocrine-disrupters, carcinogens, and mutagens, meaning they can actually break down the body's cellular defense system, causing damage to our DNA. Many chemicals used in personal care and cleaning products are industry 'secrets' and don't need to be disclosed on labels.

According to a 2018 study by the National Oceanic and Atmospheric Administration (NOAA) and the UC Davis Air Quality Research Center, personal care and industrial products are now outpacing transportation as sources of urban air pollution! NOAA atmospheric scientist Jessica Gilman explains, "gasoline is stored in closed, hopefully airtight, containers and Volatile Organic Chemicals (VOCs) in gasoline are burned for energy. Volatile chemical products used in common solvents and personal care products are literally designed to evaporate. You wear perfume or use scented products so that you can enjoy the aroma. You don't do this with gasoline." What Gilman reminds us is that while most of us may recognize that inhaling gasoline or putting it on our skin is dangerous, many common household or personal care products, due to the VOCs they also contain, carry similar yet overlooked or misunderstood risk.

In the wake of the worst wildfire and environmental disaster season the US has ever seen, these studies have been followed in 2019, by a flood of irrefutable research showing a causal connection between air pollution, including in-door air pollution, and a host of diseases. This long list includes: asthma, heart disease, depression and suicidality (especially in children and young adults), neurological diseases like MS, Parkinson, and Alzheimer's and diabetes.

Bayer-Monsanto, makers of the herbicide glyphosate, otherwise known as Round-Up, graces headlines weekly as it faces nearly 18,000 lawsuits for denying its knowledge that their herbicide causes cancer. This includes mounting evidence that the mega-corps has aggressively suppressed this research for years.

The Bayer-Monsanto example exposes the biggest problem our communities must face: that we have built much of our culture of self-care and daily life routines on the lies of corporate polluters. It is people with environmental injuries and illnesses that bear the heaviest burden of these lies.

Many people with environmental injury and illnesses, such as Multiple Chemical Sensitivity, face great difficulty having a public life and voice. Increasing levels of environmental and indoor air pollution, especially in urban environments, keep people with Environmental Illness and Injury (EII) isolated from many aspects of daily life. People also face incredible stigma from medical institutions. While seeking healthcare, many people with MCS or related illnesses are forced to challenge the presumption of a mental health condition that is used as a reason to dismiss their credibility when reporting on and understanding their own symptoms.

This undermines a person's human right to treatment. It is ableism at its worst, highlighting the abusive challenges many of us face in getting the care we deserve, particularly those with mental health disabilities.

This also exposes that legitimizing these toxic

exposures is deeply threatening to healthcare institutions. As the Bayer-Monsanto merger shows, in real life, there is no separation between major corporate polluters and the corporations which make billions off of medications. (Separate companies until 2016, Bayer is a big pharma corporation. Monsanto is an agro-chemical giant which also creates genetically modified seeds.) The very real business model of Bayer-Monsanto and many similar multinational corporate polluters is to guarantee a steady profit stream and captive consumers— aka 'patients'— by profiting from curing the diseases they cause.

Upon first reading these words they may sting of conspiracy, but the facts simply add up as sure as untold chemicals are accumulating in our cells and oceans. The bellies of beached whales filled with 80 lbs of plastic do not lie. Neither do our bodies. We, the toxically injured, whistle the tune of truth-telling even when the echo-location songs of our whale kin fall silent. We sing for them, we sing for you, we sing for all of humanity and the planet.

The deluge of chemicals in bodies and ecosystems may disrupt our cellular signaling, cause our nerves to sear in pain, but their reality and the resounding reality of their harm orient us to the actions we are being called upon to take.

New Crip Futures: Taking Action in Times of Climate Crisis

#1 — Listen to canaries! Accord us the dignity and respect we all deserve.

If you have friends, family (chosen or biological), colleagues or neighbors who have environmental injury or illnesses please listen to their feedback and requests regarding personal care and cleaning products, appliances, and construction materials, all of which may emit dangerous levels of indoor air pollution. This is solidarity that can literally save lives, including yours! This is a truth at the crossroads of disability and climate justice that we must learn to deeply embody and practice with patience, compassion and care for our collective liberation.

Too often people with diverse EII are treated with scrutiny, disbelief and stigma due to the widespread suppression of the true toxicity of our societies and the very real effects these toxins have on our bodies. The health of our bodies do require the disruption and adaptation of new practices, and we call people to confront harm that we are all experiencing but is being hidden from us. This is scary.

Consequently, people with EII often bear the heavy burden of frustration, anger, and pathologization, even from those we love most, along with the extreme physical challenges of our disability. These difficult reactions can be as disabling as the toxins themselves. Yet, they are often part of the process of grappling with these hard truths or the inconvenience of changing products or daily life practices in a world that is already so hard and overwhelming for most of us. When we hold all of this to the light of compassion and shared commitment for collective liberation, we can choose to listen to canaries and choose solidarity in new ways that are increasingly loving, liberatory, and environmentally transformative.

#2 — Make your home, work place, community centers, and/or places of religious/ spiritual practice low or no fragrance zones by using eco-friendly and fragrance free personal care and cleaning products. (Be sure the products you select are fragrance free by checking the ingredients. Sometimes products say they are 'naturally' scented and contain chemical fragrances).

Environmental health data is increasingly showing that personal care and industrial cleaning products are outpacing transportation in causing air pollution. Again, this is solidarity that can literally save lives, including yours! By collectively adapting greener products and practices, we can reduce toxic exposures in our workplaces and communities in a big way. This action honors the dignity and wisdom of survivors of environmental injury while preventing further injury and disease. It enables us to reduce community-wide pollution exposures in ways we can enact immediately, and it creates consumer-side pressure on corporate polluters to stop lying and start reducing the harm caused by their products and marketing.

There are great resources for going fragrance free available from the East Bay Meditation Center and Leah Lakshmi Piepzna-Samarasinha's Brownstargirl Blog - search their names with the key words "fragrance free" and to find them.

You can also learn more from Black Women for Wellness: https://www.bwwla.org and Women's Voices For the Earth: https://www.womensvoices.org/.

#3 — Organize for right to know laws, pesticide bans, or other community-wide Environmental & Disability Justice action!

We need to build a new consensus about the toxic tipping point. Engage your loved ones and communities about these facts, and come up with community-based solutions to reduce indoor and environmental air pollution. Some strategies include engaging your city, county or state to ban pesticides like glyphosate or advocating for laws like CA's California Toxic Fragrance Chemicals Right to Know Act of 2019 (SB574), which will soon be ratified.

#4 — Demand a moratorium — a complete stoppage — on new chemicals.

Over the long term, disability and climate justice communities need to unify around this demand along with our demand to cease the use of fossil fuels. It is crucial to note that the vast majority of industrial chemicals used on the planet today, including everything from pharmaceuticals and pesticides to plastics and food preservatives, have two primary historical roots: biological weapons made for WWI and WWII and fossil fuel industry by-products. (There is a lot of cross-over between the two, as well.)

The only exception to this moratorium should be chemicals that have been tested for safety and that fit new publicly generated criteria for green and just adaptive chemicals that function to heal our ecosystems rather than cause more damage or contribute to climate change. This means these 'adaptive' chemicals (borrowing disability justice's use of adaptive technologies) will need to emerge from institutions and industries based in a global "Green New Deal" or "Just Transition" rather than from current corporate polluters. Profits will go into the pockets of these green industries and benefit people and living systems, safeguarding our futures.

Prison moratoriums or moratoriums on the death penalties have long been a strategy of prison abolition movements. Green New Deal platforms, with the support of the combined forces of disability and climate justice movements— in collaboration with global indigenous rights leadership and movements for reparations— can begin now to adopt this strategy and demand. The UN has predicted that the global chemical industry, already at 50 trillion dollars, will double by 2050. If we allow this to happen, the planet will be forfeit and all life as we know it will be impossible.

#5 — Abolish for-profit healthcare in the US and globally wherever it persists. Transition all healthcare institutions to worker-owned co-ops.

The growing support of Medicare for All by the majority of the US public marks great progress. However, we need to go further. While managed healthcare systems and health insurers may talk a good talk about prevention, our society and its institutions are not set up to support wellness for anyone. Healthcare is big business and it's entangled like your worst bad hair day with corporate polluters. It is much more profitable to keep us sick. When we understand health and wellness from the lens of liberation, as an expression of freedom in our bodies and in our world, we understand that healthcare must be unshackled from profit. Until it is, people with disabilities will increasingly be left to die, and our societies will become increasingly disabling. Societies will also become increasingly incapable of meeting the basic needs to sustain human life and the lives of other species upon which our planetary ecosystems depend: from fish to bees, all currently facing massive die-offs.

We call upon cross-issue movements to demand healthcare services and structures that serve human and planetary need, halt and heal our climate crisis, and function as part of a regenerative New Green economy. Transitioning all healthcare institutions to worker-owned coops in the next 20-30 years is the best means of achieving this. In these co-ops, we envision health workers from cardiologists to Curanderas/Curanderxs caring for our communities with shared power and dignity. These coops can serve as healing justice's beating heart, resounding in our cells and communities, creating resilience-flow, rather than trickle down economies, that will enable us to remake our world.

Disability Liberated

by Patricia Berne, David Langstaff and
Aurora Levins Morales

*This poem and text below accompanied our
performance and installation in March 2015 at
the Disability Incarcerated Symposium at U.C.
Berkeley.*

Come. You. Yes, you.
Tonight we are gathering stories, ours, yours.
Each of us with our bundles of sticks, each of us
with our strands of cord.
The word in your pocket is what we need.
The song in your heart, the callous on your
heel.

Come out of the forest, the woodwork, the
shadows to this place of freedom
quilombo, swamp town, winter camp,
yucayeque
where those not meant to survive laugh and
weep together
share breath from mouth to mouth, pass cups of
water, break bread
and let our living bodies speak.

DISABILITY LIBERATED

Our history is in our bodies
what we do to breathe, how we move, the
sounds we make
our myriad shapes, our wild gestures
far outside the boundaries of what's expected
the knowledge bound into our bones, our
trembling muscles, our laboring lungs
like secret seeds tied into the hair of our stolen
ancestors
we carry it everywhere.

Come beloveds from your narrow places
from your iron beds, from your lonely perches
come warm and sweaty from the arms of lovers
we who invent a world each morning
and speak in fiery tongues.

Come you with voices like seagulls
dissonant and lovely, with hands like roots and
twigs.
Come limbs that wander and limbs like buds
and limbs heavy as stone
come breathless and swollen and weary,
fevered and wracked with pain.
Come slow and heavy, come wary and scarred,
come sweet and harsh and strong. Come
arched with pleasure, come slick with honey
come breathless with delight.

We say with our feet, with our backs and hands
no life belongs to another, our bodies are not
acreage

[Image description: A Black woman with long locs and a hairpiece crouches, centered, her strong right leg showing through a slit in her long skirt. She pours water from a beautiful conch shell into her cupped hand. Pictured: India Harville, photo ©Richard Downing, 2016.]

livestock, overhead, disposable tools.
We hum as we travel, songs heavy with maps
that lead us back to ourselves
singing you, yes you, are irreplaceable.

Here we are, and here we are fruitful
our stories flower, take wing, reproduce like
windblown seeds.
No surgeon's knife can cut the lines of spirit.
Our family tree remains.

*from "Listen, Speak" in Kindling: Writings On
the Body, by Aurora Levins Morales*

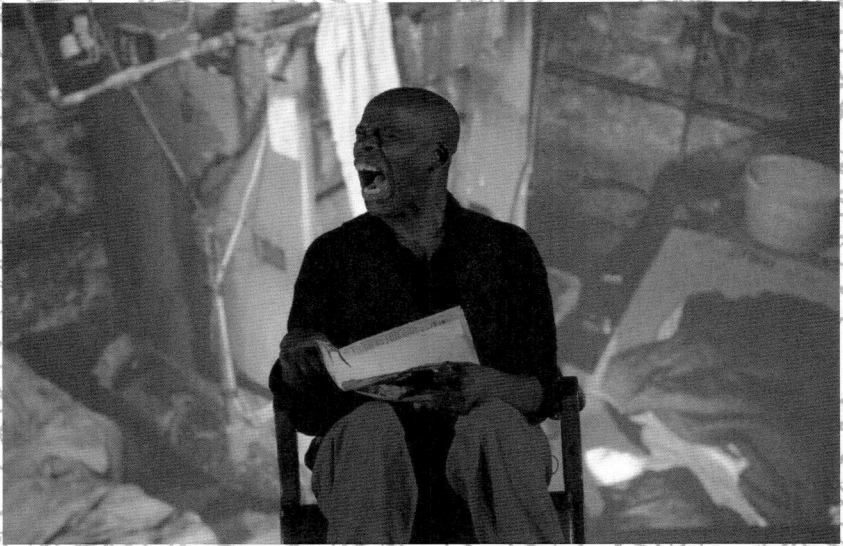

[Image description: A Black man sits in front of a projected image of horrific basement living quarters, a look of anguish on his face, mouth wide open, teeth exposed, eyes closed. He is holding a newspaper. Pictured: Leroy Moore, photo ©Richard Downing, 2015.]

Disability Liberated is not a passive grieving, but a furious mourning, an elegy to all that we have lost, and a promise to fight like hell for all that survives.

Disability Liberated was born out of collective struggle. We sought first and foremost to pay homage to the countless disabled lives that have been lost to the violence of able-bodied supremacy, whether that loss be corporeal – souls robbed of their very embodiment by state, vigilante, or, too often, intimate violence – or the loss of freedoms through incarceration in prisons or other disciplinary institutions. Our understanding of able-bodied supremacy has been formed in relation to intersecting systems of domination and exploitation. The histories of white supremacy and ableism are, after all, inextricably entwined, both forged in the crucible of colonial conquest and capitalist domination. We cannot comprehend ableism without grasping its interrelations with heteropatriarchy, white supremacy, colonialism, and capitalism, each system co-creating an ideal bodymind built upon the exclusion and elimination of a subjugated "other" from whom profits and status are extracted.

Disability Liberated keeps these connections front and center, drawing upon the legacies of cultural and spiritual resistance within vodou that confronted and subverted colonial powers along a thousand underground paths, igniting small persistent fires of rebellion in everyday life. In a historical moment in which Black communities around the country have been rising up against police violence and asserting claims to worth, dignity and power, disabled people of the global majority — Black and brown people — share common ground in our struggle for life and justice. 500+ years of violence against Black and brown bodies includes 500+ years of bodies and minds deemed dangerous by being non-normative – "deviant," "unproductive," "invalid." We know that there has always been resistance to all forms of oppression, as we know through our bones that there have simultaneously been disabled people visioning a world where we flourish, that values and celebrates us all in our diverse beauty.

Disability Liberated is an intervention into a landscape of absences. For if the ruthless violence of able-bodied supremacy were not bad enough, we also find ourselves confronted with the myriad ways in which ableism renders this violence invisible. Seldom do we find mainstream discussions of the fact that people with disabilities are disproportionately subjected to police violence, nor do we hear of the scores of children with disabilities that are abused, neglected, even caged as unhuman, murdered by their families or "caregivers" for failing to perform able-bodiedness. Similarly invisible is the callous herding of people with disabilities into jails, prisons, and institutions such as "nursing homes," "psychiatric facilities," and "rehabilitation centers" that the volume *Disability Incarcerated* rightly names as sites of segregation and confinement within a vast and growing "carceral archipelago." Just as we can trace the origins of the police to slave patrols, the coercive warehousing of people with disabilities and the rampant violence visited upon us today is rooted in eugenics, forced sterilization, and outright genocide.

"Disability Justice comes with having the ability to be pushed by others, to challenge yourself about who makes up your community, your family, your extended family, about your openness to challenge yourself and be open to bringing it to the next level so you can see your broader community. It takes a lot of being challenged and being open to have arguments and still be friends, or still be an ally to a community, moving from the 'I' to the 'we,' moving from identity politics to 'we.'"
– Leroy Moore

Our Saucy Selves: Disability Justice & Sexuality

An Interview with Patty Berne and NEVE, conducted by Cory Silverberg

So how is Disability Justice related to sexuality?

PB: Most justice based movements don't actually address the lived experience of the body, they address an archetypal idea of a body. Of course in justice movements we address demographics, but we address bodies as an abstraction, not in real time, in complex and realistic ways — what we need and offer as people who parent, or as people older than 40, as people with disabilities, as people that are overworked, or as people who don't have access to food or don't have time to eat because we're holding down 3 gigs.

Disability Justice is a practice and a framework in which disability is understood both as an

[Image description: A Black man wearing knee pads and sneakers smiles, standing, flanked on the left and right by a white man with facial complexities and an East Asian woman with two fingers on each hand and two toes on each foot. They are holding him up. All three are wearing black tank tops and shorts. Pictured: Matthew Blanchard, Lateef McLeod, Chun-Shan "Sandie" Yi, photo ©Richard Downing, 2011.]

embodied experience and a socially constructed experience. When we were initially framing disability justice (DJ) we wanted to make sure we reflected the practice elements, that DJ was not put out as just a collection of ideas and hypotheticals set in lyrical language but that it had a practice which respected the ways in which disabled people with multiple ways of being in the world could engage in movement building. And the robustness of our lives includes our sexualities.

One of the ways that disabled people are oppressed is through the negation of our sexualities as a means of denying the viability of our bodies, including our potential reproductive viability. We can see this through directly eugenic policies like "assisted suicide" (which is complex, I know) and through the general public dread of what it means to expose the nude disabled body. We started Sins Invalid with the understanding that sexuality anchors us into conversations about the body and of our embodiment.

My experience of people in their power, including people with non-normative or non-conforming bodies, is that we are hot — super hot in fact! It's super sexy to see people engaged with their lives, doin' themselves!

N: I'm moved by that piece about negating our sexuality as a means of denying our bodies' viability. It's negating our agency, our ability to make choices, and our right to make choice! An important point of intersection between DJ and sexuality is the issue of choice. I think about reproductive justice and eugenics, and wonder about people's question of whether people with developmental disabilities can consent to sex. Having a DJ lens about sexuality and consent is incredibly important because it centers the full humanity of the disabled person. It's like being asked the question: How do you have sex in a wheelchair, how does your wheelchair play into sex? I mean, I love wheelchairs, and I love to see them in porn or cinema or performance art. But I'm looking for disabled PEOPLE, not wheelchairs. It tells us that people don't understand disability experience, and that the metaphor of the wheelchair as a symbol is taken literally.

I think a lot about what is the actual intersection between DJ and sexuality, and it is not just about the tools we use to access sex or the tools we use to make the world more accessible to us. DJ is a framework through which we can be more consensual in accessing sex, it's a better way to approach sex, better than an ableist combative gendered heteropatriarchal approach to sex, or a patriarchal rape culture or hook-up culture to access sex.

What's so awesome and amazing about DJ as it's been laid out is that it's inherently intersectional as a framework and movement. So we're working with feminism and gender justice, we are thinking about immigrant justice and land rights and indigenous sovereignty and rights to agency and consent and choice. And communication of access needs for all disabled people all the time. So liberation in the context of DJ includes the right to sexual pleasure and choice and desire for all types of disabled people.

There is an attitude in white supremacist, heteropatriarchal, ableist culture towards sex and sexuality that we are combatants in a war of sex. There's an idea that we have to almost trick each other into sexual success, and I think that really sucks — not in a good way — that we have to communicate in a coded dance that's not accessible to everyone. The goal is not to communicate what you want and need, what you're up for and down for, whether for yourself or another person. DJ practiced in a sexual context advocates for communication that works for everyone around sexual desire and what we do when we're sexual.

What do immigrant rights have to do with sex?

N: For me what land rights have to do with sexuality and disability is that we are living in rape culture and a settler colonial culture, and they're not distinct, they are the same culture.

This culture is founded upon the mistaken belief that white cis heterosexual able bodied men have the right to own, rape and pillage the land and bodies of indigenous people, of all people who are not white cis heterosexual able bodied men, in a competition amongst white cis heterosexual able bodied men in pursuit of the accumulation of power.

How we treat the land is how we treat each other. How we understand who this land belongs to is how we understand who our bodies belong to. When we operate on the assumption that colonialism and imperialism are best, we also operate on the assumption that rape and non-consent are best.

PB: Yes, yes, yes and a big Fuck No to the colonial settler values based on violence and the ripple effects of colonial settler psychology!

How is sex with a disabled person the same or different than sex with a non-disabled person?

PB: Sex is different every time you have sex, and different with every different person you have sex with. Maybe what's being asked here is, is it worth the effort to have sex with a disabled person, is it worth the effort or the risk? Can I please them, will they please me?

N: Will I learn things about their body or my body that will freak me out and forever change my attitude toward sex? People think there is a standard for sex. That it is both vanilla and acrobatic, that it is spontaneous and insidiously communicated, that it could accidentally or on purpose result in the production of embryos. That it is consensual, people want it, but are not supposed to have to communicate that they want it or understand that their partner wants it.

PB: Good sex does not equal the heteropatriarchal understanding of sex, with an off the shelf penis, off the shelf vagina, straight off the porn rack, with anyone — and certainly not with a disabled person!

Is the term "disabled sexuality" useful in any context?

PB: I don't know about that term, but the term crip sex resonates for me, just as queer sexuality does, in that it implies consciousness of non-normative bodies and non-normative expressions of sexuality.

N: So this is a trick question in that DJ as framework for one's life would help a person NOT ask that question in the same way [laughter]. The major difference between having sex with a disabled person and a non-disabled person is that with a disabled person you can't make assumptions. You have to ask questions. You have to be prepared that whatever ingrained or assumed outcome you imagine (say everyone getting completely naked, or having an orgasm) is not going to happen for everyone, and also that not everyone wants it. You have to be willing to let go of expectations and come up with new possibilities. Because really, ableism can happen in a sexual interaction between a disabled person and a non-disabled person. It's possible to be ableist in bed.

But in terms of tips and techniques, the tip is communicate, ask questions, get consent, learn new things!! Pleasure looks different for different people.

What do you want people to know and understand about disability and sexuality?

N: I get asked this all the time, because so much of my work is in the realm of sexuality, and since I'm disabled, people assume that I have a message to convey. People even ask "What do you want to prove?" I like having sex and I want to keep having it and I like having it publicly. I think what I do want to convey about disability and sexuality is that neither are an anomaly, and they aren't an anomaly when they occur at the same time. I mean, we're taught to think of disability as an anomaly, but in reality disabled people are the largest group of marginalized people on earth. And it's incredible that we have this idea of disability as singular and rare and personal, but really we should be understanding disability as a huge social concept. It should be understood that when you say disability and sexuality you are speaking about very very broad topics. I would love to see disability and sexuality as broad topics, as opposed to some narrow niche understanding of human experience.

NEVE is a freelance choreographer, writer, and multidisciplinary performer. They are a collective member of Playthey Studios and Access-Centered Movement, and they have been a Sins Invalid family member since 2010. NEVE identifies as Black/Indigenous Sudanese, Scottish/white, biqueer, nonbinary, a trash femme, disabled/cripped, a country punk, and a Jersey girl. You should never mess with them but you can always fucks with them. NEVE lives in Unceded Coast Salish Duwamish Territories/ Seattle with their husbian and queer family. patreon.com/nevebebad, nevebebad.com, and @nevebebad on everythang.

PATRICIA BERNE is a Co-Founder, Executive and Artistic Director of Sins Invalid. Berne's training in clinical psychology focused on trauma and healing for survivors of interpersonal and state violence. Her professional background includes offering mental health support to survivors of violence and advocating for LGBTQI and disability perspectives within the field of reproductive genetic technologies. Berne's experiences as a Japanese-Haitian queer disabled woman provides grounding for her work creating "liberated zones" for marginalized voices. She is widely recognized for her work to establish the framework and practice of disability justice.

[Image description: photograph of Sins Invalid co-founder Patty Berne. She looks directly at the camera, and wears black glasses and dark lipstick.]

Timelines

About these Timelines

Disability justice history does not start in the 1980s when disability studies entered the academy. Crips have been resisting for hundreds of years. It is important to us to create public knowledge of the history of resistance of disabled people of color and queer and trans disabled people. This is a pushback against our historic erasure due to intersecting systems of oppression.

It is a strange experience to be the deciders of what is important enough to be documented in a timeline of resistance. This is something that, historically, disabled people of color and queer and

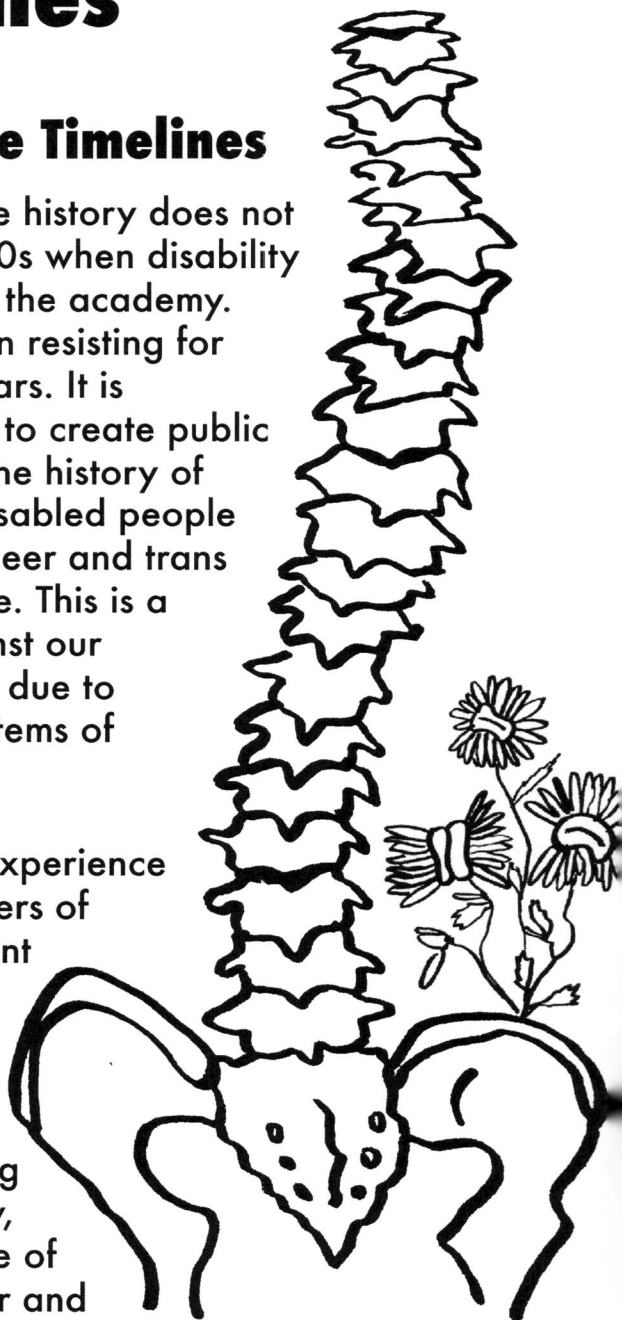

trans disabled people have not had the opportunity to do. Gathering these histories has not been an easy task, especially because so many of our stories have been lost due to our erasure. We decided to ask our community for help. We asked "what would you include in a timeline of disability justice?"

This timeline is not a reflection of the mainstream disability rights movement. Disability justice is a movement of intersections; it is not a "single issue movement." The history of Sins Invalid has also been largely influential in the movement, so some of our own contributions are reflected in the disability justice timeline as well. It's also important to note that this is not a history of the ways disabled people of color and queer and trans disabled people have experienced oppression — this is a history of resistance.

This disability justice timeline does not include the entire history of our people. We acknowledge there are gaps, especially in international perspectives. Even though we crowd-sourced events on the timeline, our reach only goes so far, and we need the input of other disabled BIPOC and people engaging in disability justice to help build it. This is only a beginning.

If you have a piece of history to add, we have created a crowd-sourced timeline that you can contribute to on our website, at sinsinvalid.org/timelines.

We also created a separate timeline to share the history of Sins Invalid. Where did we come from? How have we expanded and contracted over the years? Who have we collaborated with? We compiled the history of our organization and are offering a condensed version of it here. If you want more, there is a much more detailed and dense timeline of the history of Sins Invalid housed on our website, also available at sinsinvalid.org/timelines.

Come, learn our histories.

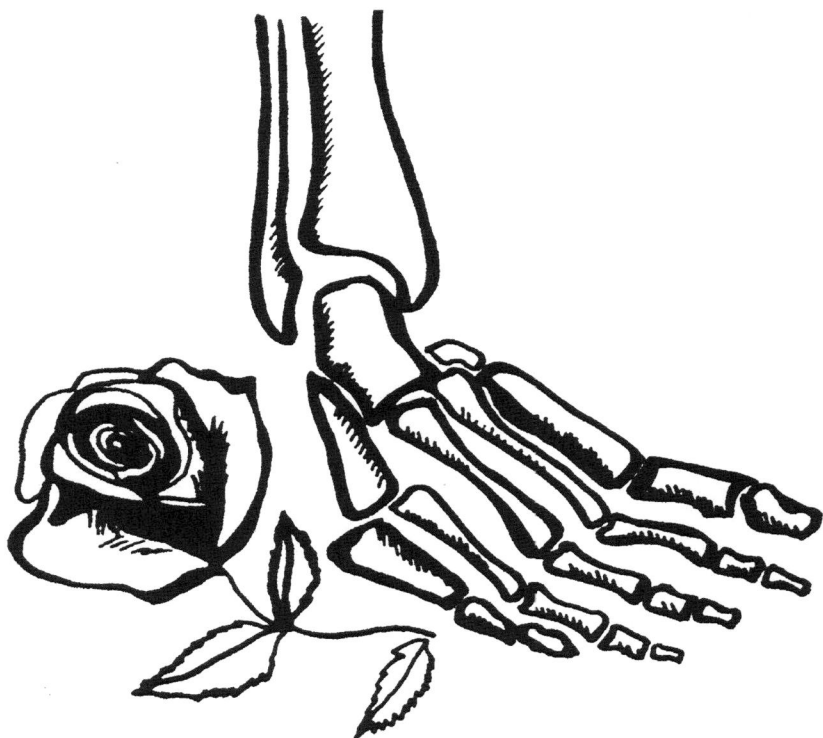

Disability Justice Timeline

1820	Harriet Tubman, conductor of the Underground Railroad, is born. She later acquired multiple disabilities, which were direct results of enslavement.
1907	Frida Kahlo, Mexican revolutionary artist, is born. She acquired multiple disabilities throughout her life and created much of her art from bed.
1955	Rebellion at Texas Hospital for the Negro Insane, lead by 19 year-old Ben Riley.
1977	Disability rights activists stage a 26 day long sit-in at SF Health, Education, and Welfare office with big help from Oakland Black Panther Party and ASL interpreters. This is now referred to as the 504 sit-ins.
1980	Creation of the National Black Deaf Advocates.
1980	Audre Lorde publishes "The Cancer Journals."

1987	Gloria Anzaldua writes about illness in the context of multiple oppressions.
1987	ACT UP (AIDS Coalition to Unleash Power) is established.
1988	"Dykes, Disability, and Stuff," created by two Jewish lesbians, Catherine Odette and Sarah Karon in Boston, begins publication.
1989	Cherríe Moraga, Chicana feminist writer and co-editor of "This Bridge Called My Back: Writings by Radical Women of Color," stages the first production of her play Heroes and Saints, which links themes of revolutionary queer Chicana identity, disability, and motherhood.
1994	Roland Johnson, leader of Speaking for Ourselves, a civil rights organization run by people with developmental disabilities, and survivor of institutionalization, releases his memoir "Lost in a Desert World."
1996	Intersex activists picket the American Academy of Pediatrics in Boston in protest of medically unneccesary surgeries on intersex children.

1998	NOLOSE founded by Dot Nelson-Turner, a disabled superfat queer trans person.
1999	Asians and Pacific Islanders with Disabilities of California is founded as an informal coalition of individuals, community-based organizations, government agencies, parent organizations, and corporate executives who shared a common vision of wanting to address the specific needs of Asians with Pacific Islanders with disabilities.
1999	Eli Clare publishes "Exile and Pride."
2000	Queer Women of Color Media Access Project is founded.
2001	Emi Koyama, a disabled Asian American activist and writer who works with the Student Hookers Association, publishes "Instigations from the Whore Revolution: A Third Wave Feminist Reponse to the Sex Work 'Controversy'" zine during a radical-feminist anti-prostitution demonstration in Portland, Oregon.
2002	The People of Color and Mixed-Race Caucus release a statement at the Queer Disability Conference.

2006	Sins Invalid's first show.
2006	Creation of the Disabled Young People's Collective.
2006	Christopher Bell publishes statement highlighting pervasive white supremacy within disability studies in 2nd edition of Disability Studies Reader.
2007	Colin K Donovan and Qwo Li Driskill publish "Scars Tell Stories" zine, a collection of writing by many sick and disabled QT/BIPOC authors.
2007	Leroy starts Krip-Hop Nation, an organization that focuses on disabled musicians.
2009	Quippings: Disability Unleashed is formed in Australia.
2009	Karen Hampton creates the Lesbians with disabilities quilt.
2009	Allied Media Conference Disability Justice track.
2009	Azolla Story created as online space for sick and disabled Asian and Pacific Islander American women and girls.
2009	Krip-Hop's first conference on Homo-Hop & Krip-Hop at UC Berkeley.

2010	Creating Resources for Empowerment in Action (CREA), a feminist human rights organization based in New Dehli, India, offers its first "Disability, Sexuality and Rights Online Institute," a recurring 6-week course on disability and sexuality.
2010	Nonbinary Mizrahi disabled organizer and writer Billie Rain creates the Sick and Disabled Queers Facebook group.
2010	Mia Mingus, Stacey Milbern and Leah Lakshmi Piepzna-Samarasinha create "Creating Collective Access" prior to the Allied Media Conference/ USSF, as a place for sick and disabled POC to find each other and collaborate on access by and for disabled POC. It happened again in 2011 and 2012, organized by other SDQTPOC including A'ishah Amatullah, Billie Rain, Rachel Gadd-Nelson and Savannah Logsdon-Breakstone.
2010	Leah Lakshmi Peipzna-Samarasinha publishes "Fragrance Free Femme of Color Realness/Genius," becomes BIPOC chemical access resource widely used.

2011	"Sick and Disabled Queer and Trans People of Color and Mixed-Race People" Facebook group is created as an offshoot of the 2010 "Sick and Disabled Queers" Facebook group.
2011	Lydia X.Z. Brown creates Autistic Hoya, an intersectional autistic space.
2011	NYC based care collectives begin to emerge and spread out.
2012	Sins Invalid launches its first international performance in Toronto, organized in large part by Black trans disabled artist Syrus Marcus Ware.
2012	D-Center (Disability and d/Deaf Cultural Center) founded through community activism by queer and POC disabled people at University of Washington.
2013	Sins Invalid documentary is released and begins touring the festival circuit, with the premiere in Osaka, Japan.
2013	Aurora Levins Morales publishes "Kindling."

2014	Syrus Marcus Ware and Leah Lakshmi Piepzna-Samarasinha co-found PDA (Performance/Disability/Art) in Toronto. P/D/A creates a disability justice artist residency, culminating in "Crip Your World" performances.
2014	Sins Invalid speaks out in solidarity with Palestine in response to pinkwashing advertising campaigns at the Vancouver Queer Film Festival.
2014	Queer Women of Color Media Access Project adopts a fragrance-free policy.
2015	NOLOSE conference has BIPOC only day with cross ability QTBIPOC organizing.
2016	The Harriet Tubman Collective, founded by 17 Black disabled activists, makes statement asking Black Lives Matter activists and Movement for Black Lives to address ableism in their movements.
2016	First Disability Intersectionality Summit.
2016	Kay Ulanday Barrett publishes "When the Chant Comes."
2016	National Coalition for Latinxs with Disabilities is formed.

2016	Disabled Bolivians journey across Andes mountains in wheelchairs and on foot to La Paz to speak with president Evo Morales about ableism. When Morales refuses to discuss their requests, protestors suspend themselves from the city's bridges.
2017	Trans Life + Liberation Art Opening, Oakland.
2017	Lydia X. Z. Brown, E. Ashkenazy, and Morénike Giwa Onaiwu publish "All the Weight of Our Dreams: On Living Racialized Autism."
2017	Bay Area Disability Community Rising in Protest and Power (BAD CRIPP) is founded.
2018	Autistic People of Color Fund launches on 1yr anniversary of "All The Weight of Our Dreams." Partnership between Autistic Women & Nonbinary Network and Lydia X.Z. Brown for community reparations for autistic people of color's interdependence, survival, and empowerment.
2018	Leah Lakshmi Piepzna-Samarasinha publishes "Care Work: Dreaming Disability Justice."

Sins Invalid Timeline

1999	Leroy Moore and Patty Berne meet at Disability Advocates of Minorites Organization (DAMO).
2004	Patty leaves her role as Project Director on Disability, Race and Eugenics at the Center for Genetics and Society, dreaming of disability centered work that highlights wholeness.
2005	Leroy Moore, Patty Berne, Todd Herman, and Amanda Coslor begin meeting in Patty Berne's living room to plan a live performance entitled "Sins Invalid" focusing on disability and sexuality.
2006	The "Sins Invalid" show is held at Brava Theater in San Francisco.
2007	Sins Invalid broadens its scope beyond performance and becomes a formal organization to continue doing cultural work around disability and sexuality.
2007	Produces second performance at Brava Theater in San Francisco.
2007	Begins filming a documentary film about Sins Invalid's work.
2008	Produces a third performance at Brava Theater in San Francisco.

2008	Creates Artistic Core to help shape the direction of the organization with Patty Berne, Leroy Moore, Elaine Beale, Vanessa Huang, and Nomy Lamm.
2008	Patty Berne, Mia Mingus, and Stacey Milbern engage in conversations about the work being done by queer disabled people of color and come up with a new framework of disability justice.
2009	Produces a fourth performance at Brava Theater in San Francisco.
2009	Participates in multiple conferences on college campuses and within communities in San Francisco, Detroit, Davis, Berkeley, and San Rafael.
2010	The Disability Justice Collective (DJC) becomes its own organization and leads a disability justice track for the 2010 Creating Change Conference.
2010	Pilots an Artists in Residence (AIR) program with emerging LGBTQI & POC disabled artists who collaborate over nine months to create content for a performance, directed by Nomy Lamm.
2010	Receives press coverage on Pacifica's Democracy Now, the New York Times, and several other independent and mainstream media outlets.

2011	Produces "Knotting Stories Across Time and Geography" performace at Z Space in San Francisco.
2011	Launches Making Connections, a series of conversations to create cross-pollination between movements.
2011	Begins relationship with Catalyst Project, providing disability justice training in exchange for anti-racist training for white people involved with Sins Invalid.
2011	Hosts performance workshops on new media and dance.
2012	First international performance in Toronto with both live performers and media artists.
2012	Collaborates on two short films: "I Cannot Speak Without Shaking" and "The Chili Story."
2012	Hosts two Making Connections conversations on the capitalist construction of disability and medicalizing 'transgressive' bodies.
2013	Completes the Sins Invalid documentary and joins New Day Films, a member-owned cooperative and the largest distributor of documentaries to the academic market.

2013	Withdraws from collaboration with the Frameline Film Festival to show solidarity with the Palestinian call for Boycott, Divestment, and Sanctions (BDS).
2013	Hosts Making Connections conversation on disability and spirituality.
2014	Chooses to withdraw from participation in the Vancouver Queer Film Festival after learning of a Pinkwashing ad in the festival's program. (Pinkwashing is the practice of aligning LGBT events with Israeli government support, and is a clear violation of the Palestinian call for BDS.) After a series of conversations, Sins Invalid releases a statement of solidarity with the Palestinian movement for human rights, including a graphic and video identifying connections between disability justice and Palestinian liberation. Rather than canceling the trip to Vancouver, Patty Berne and other Sins artists travel to B.C. for a series of alternate events including a panel, film screening, and disability justice community building sessions.

2014	Patty Berne travels to Osaka, Japan for the world premiere of the Sins Invalid documentary. The film begins touring the film festival circuit both within the United States and abroad.
2014	Starts convening of national Disability Justice Conversations with movement leaders from around the United States.
2014	Releases statement opposing police violence to coincide with the Stop Urban Shield rally and noise demo in Oakland, California.
2015	Participates in the Disability Incarcerated Symposium at UC Berkeley with "Disability Liberated: Mourn the Dead and Fight Like Hell for the Living" performance and altar-building.
2015	Organizes convening with the Disability Justice Collective in Seattle, WA to strengthen existing relationships, share experiences, and strategize together.
2016	Releases "Skin, Tooth, and Bone", also known as the Disability Justice Primer, a collection of disability justice focused essays, poetry, and foundational ideas.

2016	Produces "Birthing, Dying, Becoming Crip Wisdom" performance and "Crip Bed Life" visual art exhibit at ODC theater in San Francisco.
2017	Starts Crip Bits livestream series, an every-other-month talk show on Facebook Live, in which Patty Berne and guests talk about issues facing disability communities.
2017	Organizes "Strengthening Disability Justice in the Trump Years" conversation series with disability justice community members across the United States.
2017	Begins partnership with San Francisco Women Against Rape to increase SFWAR's capacity to serve D/deaf and Disabled survivors. Includes the launch of an annual support group program for survivors with disabilities and visual art depicting disabled community members.
2017	Writes and releases a statement about resisting white terror in response to the white supremacist rally in Charlottesville.

2018	Co-produces an outreach campaign to raise visibility of disabled survivors of sexual violence by placing posters in various Bay Area transit hubs.
2018	"What will your body say when you're free" is taught by NEVE & Leah Lakshmi Piepzna-Samarasinha in Seattle.
2018	Provides disability justice and anti-ableism trainings to community organizations, including Health Justice Commons, Forward Together, San Francisco Women Against Rape, and the Immigrant and Refugee Community Organization.

"Disability Justice has a wide entry point. I can talk about disability justice with anyone, it gives us a way for all of us to be in conversation and try to figure out how we meet each others' needs without burning out or exploiting anyone."
– Akemi Nishida

Glossary

In our dedication to disability justice and cross-disability solidarity, it is both a pleasure and a challenge to work towards accessibility in all things, including language. This glossary includes many of the words that are found in this DJ primer, with our attempt to explain what is meant by them. Of course so many of these definitions are based on our relationship to an able-bodied norm, and as language develops and is redefined, it's likely that many of these terms will become outdated by the time this book makes its rounds. The definitions included here reflect our current understanding of the usage of these words, and are offered in the spirit of making the language in this text more accessible.

Ableism
The system of discriminatory practices and beliefs that maintain and perpetuate disability oppression.

Ableist Privilege
The benefits which an ableist society gives to people based on conforming to a set of norms of physical, mental, psychological functioning.

Able-Bodied
People who are not physically disabled.

Able-Bodied Normativity
The expectation that everybody is able-bodied, and that being able-bodied is normal.

Able-Bodied Supremacy
A system that reinforces the superiority of non-disabled people.

Able-Minded
Similar to Able-Bodied, refers to people who don't have mental health disabilities, psych impairments, developmental disabilities, learning disabilities, etc.

(The) Academy
Higher education, a place of study or training; academia.

Access Needs/Accessibility
Access needs are those things that are needed in order for someone to fully participate in a space or activity, which can include wheelchair access, scent-free space, ASL interpretation, etc. In a disability justice context, access needs are seen as universal - every bodymind has needs, not just disabled people.

Accommodations
Adaptations for individual people based on their specific (sometimes called "special") needs.

Accountability
Obligation or willingness to be held responsible for one's actions.

Adaptive Technology
Versions of already existing technologies or tools that provide enhancements or different ways of interacting, in order to support people with disabilities in accomplishing tasks.

Advocacy Organizations
Groups that work for the interests of specific populations, and which aim to influence decisions within political, economic and social systems and institutions, including media campaigns, public speaking, publishing research, lobbying, etc.

Alignment
A position of agreement or alliance. Being "in line" with.

Ally
Someone who helps or supports someone else; often refers to people who are not a part of an oppressed group but who work to support the liberation of those people, i.e. anti-racist white people, queer-supporting straight people, etc.

Archetypal
An almost god-like model or idea of how a certain thing should be, which people, ideas and structures are assumed to be reflections of.

Assisted Suicide
Suicide committed with assistance from another person, often a doctor.

Audiocentric
Believing that people who can hear (or behave in the manner of those who can hear) are superior to those who can't or don't.

Audiocentric Privilege
Benefits given to those who can navigate a culture or society centered around the ability to hear.

Audism
Oppression based on the assumption that all people should navigate the world as hearing people do.

Authenticity
The quality of being genuine and true to oneself.

Autonomy
Independence, freedom; the ability to be self-governing, to make decisions for oneself.

BIPOC
Black, Indigenous, & People of Color.

Bodymind
The relationship between the human body and mind as a single integrated entity. This term is used instead of saying "body and mind" to affirm the reality that our minds and bodies cannot be separated.

Boycott, Divestment & Sanctions (BDS)
Palestinian-led campaign promoting various forms of boycott against Israel until the nation-state meets its obligations under international law, including withdrawal from occupied territories, removal of the separation barrier in the West Bank, full equality for Palestinian citizens of Israel, and the rights of Palestinian refugees to return to their homes and properties.

Broad-Based Popular Movement
A large group of people with a common ideology or agenda who try together to achieve certain general goals.

Capitalism
An economic system in which certain people or companies own the majority of the wealth and resources, and are able to make decisions that impact those who need money, food, shelter, etc. In capitalism, the world is divided

into two categories: those who have things/ those who want things; those who sell things/ those who buy things. One common feature of capitalism is a high level of competition; the idea that there isn't enough to go around and that you have to fight to get what you need, by being better/faster/smarter/stronger than other people.

Capitalist Domination

A system in which people and companies who own resources within the system of Capitalism have control or influence over people's lives and ability to survive.

Carceral Archipelago

Literally, a prison made up of a series of islands. The Carceral Archipelago refers to the employment of physical boundaries in order to gain control of public space, often using walls, gates, fences, surveillance cameras and security checkpoints to control a population, discouraging public gatherings and keeping outsiders from passing through. This is a reference to the work of philosopher Michel Foucalt.

Chattel Slavery

A system in which human beings are owned by other people, and forced to work for nothing. Chattel slavery means that people are considered to be complete property and will be treated as slaves forever, including their children and children's children, and can be bought and sold at will. Enslaved people in this system have no say over the direction of their own lives. In the United States, enslaved African people (along with exploited immigrant labor and the extermination and relocation of Indigenous populations) built much of the infrastructure that led to the US domination of the world economy.

Chemical Injury

Similar to Multiple Chemical Sensitivities and Scent Sensitivities, these are impairments in which people's exposure to chemicals and fragrances have caused ongoing cumulative injury and disability.

Chronic Illness

Long-term, ongoing health conditions that impact people's pain levels, energy levels, and abilities.

Cis

Also "cisgender." A term created by trans and gender non-conforming communities to describe people whose gender corresponds with the sex they were assigned at birth. The term is helpful to de-center gender normativity, but it has been critiqued for erasing intersex bodies and the process of intersex medicalization.

Civil Rights
Guarantees of equal social opportunities and protections under the law, including the right to vote, the right to a fair trial, the right to access services, the right to public education, and the right to use public facilities.

Classism
Oppression based on social or economic class, including attitudes, behaviors, policies and practices set up to benefit those with access to wealth, at the expense of poor and working class people.

Cognitive Impairments
Variations that impact brain function, sometimes temporarily, including "brain fog," memory loss, traumatic brain injury (TBI), and dementia. Sometimes cognitive impairments are the result of "flare-ups" from other disabilities, including migraines, Multiple Sclerosis (MS), diabetes, and chronic pain.

COINTELPRO
The "Counter Intelligence Program," a series of secret, often illegal projects conducted by the US Federal Bureau of Investigation (FBI) between 1956-1971, aimed at surveilling, infiltrating, discrediting, and disrupting political organizations deemed "subversive," including feminists, anti-war activists, communists, Black Power and Civil Rights Movement organizers, Puerto Rican Independence activists, and the American Indian Movement.

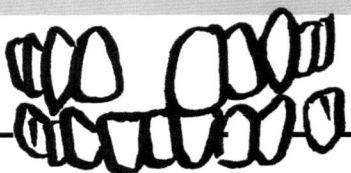

"Even the idea that control is something we need to have over our bodies, or over anything... it's puritanical... the idea that we're supposed to restrict our food appetite, and our sexual appetites, and everything to be this one idealized type of body that doesn't actually exist... we're all culturally pressured to aspire to that."
—Caleb Luna

Colonialism
The formal process of an organized group or government taking land, resources, medicine, histories, and body- and land-autonomy away from the existing Indigenous peoples.

Colonial Conquest
Engaging in colonialism as an act of war; the act of taking over a land and people.

Commode
A chair with a hole in the seat and a pot underneath that is used as a toilet.

Components
Parts of a larger whole.

Consent
Permission for something to happen or agreement to do something.

Constituency-led Centers
Organizations for specific populations that are run by those people; i.e. Centers for Independent Living (CIL's) run by people with disabilities.

Corporeal
Relating to the body.

Crips
In-group slang for people with disabilities.

Crucible
A situation in which different elements interact, leading to the creation of something new.

Cultural-linguistic
Relating to the connection between culture and language.

Curanderas/Curandxs
Traditional Latina/Latinx healers.

D/deaf
Both a descriptor of someone's capacity for auditory hearing/processing and a cultural identity connected to Deaf community, arts, politics, and culture.

Deafhood
A term coined by Paddy Ladd that conveys a positive association with the experience of being Deaf, and the process of coming into and developing a Deaf identity throughout one's life.

Dehumanization
To view or treat someone, or groups of people, as if they aren't human, and don't have full human qualities, personalities, desires, and dignity.

Demographics
The number and characteristics of people who live in a particular area or form a particular group, especially in relation to their age, race or ethnicity, gender, and other identity factors.

Developmental Disabilities
Term used to describe disabilities which become apparent in a person's early life, when certain milestones of development related to language acquisition, speech, mobility, and other areas occur outside of the typical timeline and/or manner.

Deviant
Abnormal, atypical, or deviating from the accepted norm, often with the implication of moral failing.

Disability
Disability is a word that links people of common overlapping related experiences of oppression based in navigating a world designed and defined by able-bodied people. This term has been reclaimed by people whose bodyminds have been medicalized and pathologized, working from an empowered perspective.

Disability Bureaucratic Sector
Organizations and structures that act as gatekeepers and administrators of resources, claims, services and rights related to people with disabilities.

Disability Studies
The academic field of study related to disability.

DHoH
Deaf and Hard of Hearing.

Domination
Control over someone or something, usually through force.

Elegy
A poem of serious reflection, often for the dead.

Emergent
In the process of coming into being or becoming prominent.

Emotional Impairment or Disability
A disability that impacts a person's ability to effectively recognize, interpret, control, and express fundamental emotions. Also sometimes labeled as Emotional Disturbance or Behavioral Disability.

Environmental Injury
Harm or damage caused by factors present in our environments, including mold, smoke inhalation, radiation, pesticides, or other types of toxic exposures.

Environmental Justice
The struggle to protect the natural world, with specific attention to the perspectives of Black, Brown and Indigenous communities, who often live, work and play closest to the sources of pollution.

Epistemological
Related to the study of knowledge, belief, and how we know what we know. Epistemology asks the question: How do we know if something is a belief or a fact?

Equity
Giving everyone what they need in order to have equal opportunities. This might mean some people are given more than others in certain situations, in order to make things more fair.

Escalation

Increasing or rising, often referring to a conflict becoming more intense.

Eugenics

The practice of controlling a population by deciding who is born, who is able to have kids, who is given healthcare, and who is allowed or encouraged to die, in order to create a specific "desirable" population. Eugenics can include genetic engineering, forced sterilization and birth control, assisted suicide, and other mechanisms through which people in power get to decide who is worth existing.

Exploitation

Treating someone unfairly in order to benefit from their work.

> "A lot of people who are not fat, or who are not disabled, don't want to be either of those things. And so people will see us, and say 'I don't want to look like that, I don't want to end up like that,' and they project the bodies that they don't want to have onto our bodies..."
> — Bianca Laureano

GLOSSARY

Fascism
A political system that values an image of an idealized nation or race, led by an all-powerful ruler, with strict rules about who belongs and who doesn't, and harsh punishments for straying outside the assumed norm.

Fat Oppression
The oppression of fat bodies and fat people through medical, social, governmental and economic systems.

Female Socialized
A term to describe those who have been taught to take on social expectations and attitudes associated with being assigned female.

Framework
The supporting structure for a building or object; can also refer to the structure used to create an idea.

Gender Binary
The system that proposes that gender is made up of two distinct and opposite categories, male and female, and every person and body must fit into one category or the other.

Gender Non-conforming
Behavior or appearance that does not conform to dominant cultural and social ideas about what is appropriate to a person's gender.

Gender Normativity
The expectation that everybody should fit exclusively into the gender they were assigned at birth.

Genderqueer
Identifying outside of mainstream gender, or as a combination of traditional genders.

Green New Deal
Proposed US legislation spearheaded by Alexandria Ocasio-Cortez, to address climate chaos and economic inequality. The name refers to the New Deal, Roosevelt's response to the Great Depression. The Green New Deal combines social and economic reforms and public works projects with modern ideas such as renewable energy and resource efficiency.

Hard of Hearing
Having limited ability to hear.

Heteronormativity
A world view that promotes heterosexuality as the normal or preferred sexual orientation.

Heteropatriarchy
A system where men and heterosexuals have authority over women and people of other genders and sexual orientations.

Hierarchy
A system in which people are ranked one over another according to status or authority.

Hook-up Culture
A culture or subculture that emphasizes and values sexual encounters without including emotional bonding or long-term commitment.

Homage
Special honor or respect shown publicly.

ICE
Immigration and Customs Enforcement, an agency of the Department of Homeland Security, a branch of the United States government created under the March 2003 Homeland Security Act.

Image Description
Text that describes what is happening in a visual image, often as an accommodation for people who are Blind or sight impaired, sometimes called "alt text." Image descriptions can include composition (what is where?), style (photo or drawing?), colors, number and appearance of people, clothing styles, emotions, surroundings, and placement and transcription of text.

Impairments
Mental, emotional, or physical variations

in function (what are often referred to as disabilities).

Imperative
Necessary; not to be avoided or evaded.

Imperialism
A policy or practice of extending the power of a nation over other lands and peoples, through colonization or by gaining control over the political or economic life of another area; the extension or imposition of power, authority or influence.

Incarcerated
Imprisoned or confined, whether in jails, prisons, detention centers, ICE facilities, mental hospitals or nursing homes.

Incubated
Supported in an environment that creates conditions for survival, growth, and fulfillment of one's talent or potential.

Indigenous
Being of, arising from, or having ancestors who have always lived in a specific place; native.

Indigenous Sovereignty
The ability of indigenous people to govern themselves; freedom from colonial rule.

Institutional Power
The ability or authority to decide what its best for others, to exercise control over others, or to decide who has access to resources.

Intellectual Disabilities
Differences in thinking, and societal treatment based on these differences. These may include variations in memory, reading ability, auditory processing, ability to focus or pay attention, communication style, ability to process numbers or math, ability to understand what is happening, and learning disabilities in general.

Interdependence
The state of being dependent upon each other.

Internalized Ableism
Ableism that is played out inside ourselves which impacts our beliefs about our own worth and capacity.

Interpreter
A person who translates from one language to another, including American Sign Language (ASL).

Intersectionality
The cumulative impact of multiple forms of oppression (including racism, sexism and classism) in the experiences of marginalized individuals and groups. This term was introduced by Kimberlé Crenshaw in 1989 in

the University of Chicago Legal Forum. See Sins Invalid's "10 Principles of Disability Justice" for more information.

Intersex
Bodies that have variations of sex characteristics at birth including chromosomes, gonads, sex hormones, or genitals that can result in being targeted for medical intervention ranging from labeling and diagnosis to surgery, often at an age too young for the individual to be able to consent.

Invisibilized
Having been made invisible; having erased the voices, perspectives, and contributions of certain people.

Isolation
Being alone or separate, often not by choice.

Just Transition
A set of principles, processes and practices, developed by the Labor Movement and the Environmental Justice Movement, that build economic and political power to shift from an extractive (wasteful, exploitative) economy to a regenerative (holistic, equitable) economy.

Land Rights
Usually refers to recognition of Indigenous people's legal and ethical entitlement to land and resources.

Legal Repercussions
Punishments and restrictions that can result from matters being brought into the realm of courts, legislating bodies, law enforcement, and other legal entities.

Liaison
A person who serves as a point of contact between one group and another. For example, protestors at political actions will often identify one person to interact with police and communicate demands, expectations, needs, and responses back and forth, in order to help keep people safe.

Liberation
Becoming free.

Litigation
The process of taking legal action.

Low-stimulation Space
A room or tent intentionally set aside to offer a quiet, dimly lit environment where people can take a break from interaction, bright lights, or loud noises, in order to calm down and regulate their nervous systems.

Luminaries
Those who inspire or influence others.

Mainstreaming
The practice of putting children with disabilities into classrooms with non-disabled peers, as mandated by the Individuals with Disabilities Education Act (IDEA). There are positive and negative impacts of this legislation, including increased access to participation in mainstream culture, and loss of kinship with other disabled students.

Marginalized
A person or group who is treated as unimportant or outside the range of normal perspective or experience.

Medical Industrial Complex
A for-profit industry that decides whose body must be fixed or changed, and exists at the expense of people who have been labeled as sick, disabled, or otherwise pathologized.

Membership-based National Organizations
Groups with a specific purpose that involves connecting people together around a particular activity, identity, interest or mission, in order to encourage interaction and collaboration.

Militarization
The process of becoming ready to be engaged in conflict or war.

Mixed Ability
Different types of disabilities and access needs interacting in a context that allows people to collaborate across difference.

Mobility Impairments
Variations in ability to walk, move, or navigate spaces physically. People with mobility impairments may use assistive devices including wheelchairs, prosthetics, canes, walkers, transfer benches and lifts.

Mobilization
A politicized action; putting something into movement.

Monocultural
A way of being that only allows for the expression of a single social or ethnic group, stemming from the belief within the dominant group that their practices are superior.

Monolingual

Speaking or allowing only one language.

Multiple Chemical Sensitivity (MCS)

A disability in which people become sick from exposure to chemicals or fragrances they come into contact with.

Neurodiversity

A spectrum of variations in nervous system function related to thinking, communication, sensory processing, planning and coordinating physical movement, and more.

Neurological Disability

Disability related to the brain, spine, and/ or nervous system, including epilepsy, stroke, Parkinsons, migraines, cerebral palsy, and multiple sclerosis.

Non-Apparent Disabilities

Impairments that are not obvious or visible. Could range from food allergies to autoimmune conditions to chronic pain to mental health conditions.

Non-Binary

In the context of gender, non-binary describes the experience of not being confined to a choice between two opposite (binary) genders.

Normativity
Relating to or defining standards or norms; what is considered within the range of acceptable "normal" appearance or behavior.

Oppression
Prolonged cruel or unjust treatment, often based on identity factors including race, immigration status, gender, sexuality, age, class, or ability.

Oralism
The system of teaching D/deaf people to communicate using speech and lip-reading instead of sign language.

Paternalism
A system or attitude in which a group or individual assumes authority over other people and attempts to control, provide for, and regulate their lives under the assumption that the authority knows better what is good for them.

Pathologized
Viewed or characterized as medically or psychologically abnormal and needing to be fixed.

Patriarchy
A system of society or government that gives men power and excludes women and people of other genders from it.

Performance Art
An art form that involves a combination of spoken word, music, dance, or other types of embodiment in front of a live audience.

Philosophy of Independent Living
A way of looking at society and disability that prioritizes the ability of disabled people to choose how and where they want to live, what they do with their time and resources, and who they want to interact with.

Phonocentric
Believing that sound and verbal speech are superior to other types of language and communication.

Pinkwashing
The practice of promoting the gay-friendliness of a government or corporation in order to downplay their negative actions.

POC
People of Color.

Police Brutality
Violence committed by police.

Praxis
Theory in practice; the process of combining ideas and actions.

Prison Abolition
The elimination of the prison system, to be replaced by other systems of pursuing justice.

Prison Industrial Complex
The overlapping interests of government and corporations that use surveillance, policing and imprisonment as solutions to economic, social and political problems.

Privilege
Special rights and advantages available only to certain people or groups.

Progressive
Advocating for progress, change, improvement, or reform, as opposed to wishing to maintain things as they are, especially politically.

Pronouns
Words that are used to refer to a person, including he/him, she/her, and they/them. It is important to know what pronouns people use so that we can refer to them with the words they choose.

Psych Survivors
People who have either willingly or nonconsensually been committed to mental hospitals, been medicated for mental health reasons, or experienced other types of psychiatric intervention.

Queer

An umbrella term used by people who are lesbian, gay, bisexual, transgender, or other sexual or gender minorities to describe themselves; the term has been reclaimed from people who would use it as an insult against LGBT+ people.

Radical

Relating to or impacting the fundamental nature of something; getting to the root.

Rape Culture

A society with widespread social attitudes that normalize and trivialize sexual assault and abuse.

Reciprocity

A situation in which two or more people or groups of people offer each other support and enjoy equal benefit from the relationship.

Reproductive Justice

A term that links reproductive rights and social justice, coined by Loretta Ross of the SisterSong Women of Color Reproductive Justice Collective. Reproductive Justice addresses the ways race, gender, class, ability, and sexuality intersect and impact reproductive health and the options available.

Rights-based Framework

A system for working on issues that centers around trying to obtain certain rights or guarantees from existing power structures.

SDQTPOC

Sick & Disabled Queer/Trans People of Color.

Service Provision Agencies

Organizations that are responsible for providing services to clients, including help accessing food, housing, transportation, attendant services, and other access support.

"In societies that are based on unequal distribution of resources, on accumulation for some, it's built in that significant numbers of people will be excluded and that the justification for exclusion is based on our bodies (and sometimes our minds and cultures). For disability liberation, we take on the liberation of our bodies that undermines the body justification of all oppressions."
— Aurora Levins Morales

Sensory Disability
Variations in ability related to sight, hearing, smell, touch, or taste. Examples of sensory disabilities include people who are Blind, Deaf, who have anosmia (lack of sense of smell), and people with sensory processing disorders.

Sensory Minority
People who experience one or more of the senses in a way that is different from dominant assumptions of how sight, hearing, or other senses should work.

Settler Colonialism
A type of colonialism, or an aspect of colonialism, in which indigenous populations are displaced and replaced by an invasive population that develops a distinct identity and culture that reflects the values of the imperial/colonial government. Settler Colonialism is particularly devastating because it rarely ends.

Social Mobility
Changes in social status within a hierarchy. Ability to attain greater wealth and social status is called "upward mobility"; loss of wealth and status is known as "downward mobility."

Solidarity
Unity and mutual support amongst those who have common interests.

Subjugated
Brought under domination or control.

Surveillance
The close, constant watching of a person or people by government, military, or corporate entities.

SWANA
Southwest Asia and North Africa. This term refers to the region in geographical terms rather than the political terms defined by Europe and North America (i.e. the "Middle East").

Systemic Oppressions
Forms of discrimination and inequality that are backed by laws and policies and work together to compound negative impacts and make it difficult to fight back against them.

Transformative Justice
A strategy for responding to conflict without involving the criminal justice system. Transformative justice looks for root causes of social problems and seeks to address those rather than relying on punishment to control populations.

Transgender/Trans
A person whose gender does not correspond with the sex they were coercively assigned at birth.

Transmisogyny

Misogyny or hatred of women that specifically impacts trans women and trans-feminine people who are coercively assigned male at birth. The term was coined by writer and theorist Julia Serano in her 2007 book "Whipping Girl."

Urban Shield

A regional, national and global weapons expo and SWAT training that takes place annually in the Bay Area.

Vanilla (sex)

A term created by people whose sexual activities and relationship dynamics consciously/consensually engage with power (bondage, discipline, roleplay), pain (sadism/masochism), or specific fetishes ("kink").
The term is used to describe sex that is not considered kinky or consciously playing with power. It is usually assumed to be loving, sweet, and normative.

Vigilante

A person or organization that acts in a law enforcement capacity without legal authority, often violently.

Vodou

A Hatian religion practiced by descendents of various African ethnic groups who were enslaved and Christianized by Catholic missionaries. The word Vodou means "spirit" or "deity."

War on Drugs

A campaign of drug prohibition, military aid, and military intervention, aimed at reducing illegal drug trade in the United States. The War on Drugs has disproportionately targeted Black and brown people, leading to high rates of arrest and incarceration that have torn apart families and destabilized communities.

White Supremacy

A system built on the belief that whiteness and white people are better than everyone else, and should dominate society. This belief system can show up in both subtle and extreme ways depending on context, and is perpetuated in both our actions and inactions when we don't take time and care to challenge it.

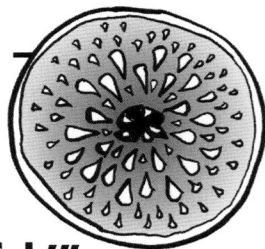

"It's really great to scrape off the ableism and patriarchy and look in the mirror and say 'whoa you're really beautiful.'"
— Patty Berne

Further Reading

Sins Invalid Social Media Channels

Facebook
https://www.facebook.com/sinsinvalid

Instagram
https://www.instagram.com/sinsinvalid

New Day (purchase our documentary)
https://www.newday.com/film/sins-invalid

Twitter
https://twitter.com/sinsinvalid

Vimeo-on-Demand (stream full performances)
https://vimeo.com/sinsinvalid/vod_pages

Website
https://sinsinvalid.org

Youtube
https://www.youtube.com/user/CripJustice

Sins Invalid Partner Organizations

Catalyst Project
https://collectiveliberation.org

Dancers Group (Sins Invalid's fiscal sponsor)
https://dancersgroup.org

Forward Together
https://forwardtogether.org

Health Justice Commons
https://healthjusticecommons.org

Movement Generation
https://movementgeneration.org

Peacock Rebellion
https://www.peacockrebellion.org

Queer Women of Color Media Access Project (QWOCMAP)
https://qwocmap.org

San Francisco Women Against Rape
https://www.sfwar.org

Sins Invalid Past and Present Artists

Alex Cafarelli
https://www.sinsinvalid.org/blog/
artists-profile-alex-cafarelli

Alli Yates
https://soundcloud.com/collander

Antoine Hunter
https://www.realurbanjazzdance.com

Aurora Levins Morales
http://www.auroralevinsmorales.com

Cara Page
https://carapage.co/about/

Damon Shuja Johnson
https://www.youtube.com/watch?v=fUXYxxj6Qnw

Elliot Kukla
https://www.nytimes.com/2018/01/10/opinion/in-
my-chronic-illness-i-found-a-deeper-meaning.html

ET Russian
https://etrussian.com

Fayza Bundalli
http://www.fayzabundalli.com

India Harville
http://lovingtheskinyouarein.com

Ines Ixierda
http://www.inesixierda.com

John Killacky
https://en.wikipedia.org/wiki/Queer_Crips

Juba Kalamka
https://jubakalamka.bandcamp.com

Kele Nitoto
https://www.facebook.com/OHDrums/

Kiyaan Abadani
https://kiyaanabadani.com

Lateef McLeod
http://www.lateefhmcleod.com

Leah Lakshmi Piepzna-Samarasinha
http://brownstargirl.org

Leroy Moore
http://kriphopnation.com
https://www.poorpress.net/product-page/krip-hop-nation
http://www.xochitljustice.org/buy-books-2/black-disabled-art-history-101

Lezlie Frye
https://transform.utah.edu/disability-studies/
faculty/

Lisa Ganser
http://facebook.com/lganser

Lisa Thomas Adeyemo
https://strozziinstitute.com/staff/
lisa-thomas-adeyemo/

Maria Palacios
https://cripstory.wordpress.com

Mat Fraser
https://www.matfraser.co.uk/p/home.html

Matthew Blanchard
https://wm.academia.edu/matthewblanchard

Micah Bazant
https://www.micahbazant.com

NEVE
https://www.nevebebad.com

Noemi Sohn
http://todaysrevolutionarywomenofcolor.com/
interviews/interview-44-noemi-sohn

Nomy Lamm
http://www.nomyteaches.com

Oriana Bolden
https://vimeo.com/projectproject

Sandie Yi
https://www.cripcouture.org

seeley quest
https://artofchangingtheworld2017.sched.com/squesting

Seema Bahl
https://www.bellevuecollege.edu/sociology/staff/seema-bahl/

Tacuma King
https://www.bayyoutharts.org

Tee Tagor
http://teetagor.portfoliobox.me/about-tagorart

Thanh Diep
https://www.creativityexplored.org/artists/thanh-my-diep

Todd Herman
https://www.toddedwardherman.com

Zahna Simon
https://dancingreenz.blogspot.com

DJ Visionaries We Admire

Akemi Nishida
https://gws.uic.edu/profiles/nishida-akemi/

Alex Lu
https://medium.com/@alexijie

Alice Wong
https://disabilityvisibilityproject.com/about/

Bianca Laureano
http://biancalaureano.com

Billie Rain
http://www.billierain.com

Bri Moore
http://www.powernotpity.com

Caleb Luna
https://www.instagram.com/chairbreaker

Cyree Jarelle Johnson
http://cyreejarellejohnson.com

Eli Clare
http://eliclare.com

Imani Barbarin
https://crutchesandspice.com

Kay Ulanday Barrett
https://www.kaybarrett.net

Kebo Drew
https://www.qwocmap.org/KeboDrew.html

Lydia X. Z. Brown
https://autistichoya.net/bio/

Mia Mingus
https://leavingevidence.wordpress.com

Dr. Paddy Ladd
http://www.deafhood.com/test/author.html

Dr. Sara Acevedo
http://bit.ly/saraacevedo

Sebastian Margaret
http://bit.ly/sebastianmargaret

Shayda Kafai
https://www.instagram.com/cripfemmecrafts

Stacey Milbern
https://twitter.com/cripchick

Syrus Marcus Ware
https://syrusmarcusware.com

Vanessa Huang
https://vanessahuang.com

Vanessa Rochelle Lewis
https://www.pleasurenesslitacademy.com

DJ Projects and Organizations We Love

Access Centered Movement
https://accesscenteredmovement.com

Autistic Hoya
https://www.autistichoya.com

Autistic Self Advocacy Network (ASAN)
https://autisticadvocacy.org

Bay Area Disability Community Rising In Power and Protest (BADCRIPP)
http://bit.ly/BADCRIPP

Black Women for Wellness
https://www.bwwla.org

Cascadia Deaf Nation
https://www.cascadiadeafnation.co/aboutourprinciples

Disability Justice Collective
http://bit.ly/DJcollective

Disability Justice Culture Club
http://bit.ly/DJculture

Disability Visibility Project
https://disabilityvisibilityproject.com

FURTHER READING

Fat Rose
https://fatrose.org

Harriet Tubman Collective
https://harriettubmancollective.tumblr.com

Krip-Hop
https://kriphopnation.com

Power Not Pity Podcast
http://www.powernotpity.com

The Body is Not an Apology
https://thebodyisnotanapology.com

[Image description: A chubby white nonbinary masculine-appearing person, arms covered with tattoos, holds a microphone. They wear a grey shirt with sparkly silver letters that says "Justice for Kayla Moore." In the background is a projection of a young black man's face (Idriss Stelley). Pictured: Lisa Ganser, photo ©Richard Downing, 2015.]

Books and Other Publications Mentioned in the DJ Timeline

All the Weight of Our Dreams: On Living Racialized Autism, edited by Lydia X. Z. Brown, E. Ashkenazy, Morénike Giwa Onaiwu, DragonBee Press, 2017

The Cancer Journals, Audre Lorde, Aunt Lute Books, 1980

Care Work: Dreaming Disability Justice, Leah Lakshmi Piepzna-Samarasinha, Arsenal Pulp Press, 2018

Dykes, Disability, and Stuff, Disabled Womyn's Educational Network, 1988-2001

Exile and Pride: Disability, Queerness, and Liberation, Eli Clare, Duke University Press, 1999

Instigations from the Whore Revolution: A Third Wave Feminist Response to the Sex Work Controversy, Emi Koyama, Confluere Pubs., 2001

Kindling: Writings on the Body, Aurora Levins Morales, Palabrera Press, 2013

Lost In A Desert World: The Autobiography of Roland Johnson, Roland Johnson & Karl Williams, Speaking for Ourselves, 1994

FURTHER READING

Scars Tell Stories: A Queer and Trans (Dis) Ability Zine, edited by Qwo Li-Driskill and Colin K. Donovan, 2007

This Bridge Called My Back: Writings by Radical Women of Color, edited by Cherrie Moraga and Gloria E. Anzaldua, Persephone Press, 1981

When The Chant Comes, Kay Ulanday Barrett, Heliotrope Books, 2016

[Image description: A fat white Jewish femme wears a painted on black curly mustache, a pink sequined headband over their dark hair, their tattooed arms extended overhead giving the "devil horns" hand signals with sequined pink wrist bands and blue fingernail polish. They are wearing a handwoven cream and blue tallis (Jewish prayer shawl) with a star of David in gold on the corner. They wear a red and brown shirt that says, "I hope I live to see the fall of the American Empire. " Pictured: Nomy Lamm, photo ©Richard Downing, 2011.]

Acknowledgments

The original vision for *Skin, Tooth, and Bone* and the foundation of this work comes from Patty Berne, and her collaborations with Leroy Moore. Most of the text in this primer was originally written by Patty Berne, with support from David Langstaff, Aurora Levins Morales, Nomy Lamm and Stacy Milbern. Much of the material was developed collectively over time, with participation from Leroy Moore, Kiyaan Abadani, Lateef McLeod, Micah Bazant, Eden Amital, NEVE, Leah Lakshmi Piepzna-Samarasinha, Maria Palacios, seeley quest, and more.

After the original publication of the Disability Justice Primer in 2016, we collected input from community members including E.T. Russian, seeley quest, Evelyn Shen, Shayda Kafai, Leah Lakshmi Piepzna-Samarasinha and Malcolm Shanks. This feedback was synthesized and integrated with support from India Harville and Caitlin Carmody.

The Second Edition of *Skin, Tooth, and Bone* has been edited and compiled by Nomy Lamm, with support from Sofia Webster, as well as Andraéa LaVant, Gordon Brown, Rafi Darrow, Yema Yang, Karina Camarera Heredia, Haley Parsley, Blair Webb, Lisa Ganser (influenced by their work with POOR Magazine and the Idriss Stelley Foundation), and Bianca Laureano, with big picture editing support from Cory Silverberg.

ACKNOWLEDGMENTS

New sections for this primer were written and edited by Ashanti Monts-Tréviska, Zahna Simon, Rei Ga-wun Leung, Dany Ko (the Audism and Deafhood Section), Mordecai Cohen Ettinger and the Health Justice Commons (Call to Action from Survivors of Environmental Injury).

Layout & design by Max Airborne.

Art throughout the primer by Micah Bazant.

Photos by Richard Downing.

Cover art and illustrations by Nomy Lamm.

[Image description: The layout throughout this primer is supplemented by drawings of bones, skin cells, mutated flowers, a deer with a small leg, bees, octopus tentacles, a bent spine, and teeth of various humans, non-human primates, eels, alligators, and other creatures. These graphics illustrate the elements of Skin, Tooth, and Bone as they relate to our images, quotes, and frameworks. They also illustrate our membership in the larger family of beings on this planet, whose futures are all bound up together.]